TRUE
ESCAPE
STORIES

TED SMART

First published in 2001 by Usborne Publishing Ltd,
Usborne House, 83-85 Saffron Hill, London
EC1N 8RT, England.
www.usborne.com

A catalogue record for this title is available from
the British Library

ISBN 07460 5761 X

Printed in Great Britain

Based on *Tales of Real Escape* by Paul Dowswell
Edited by Jenny Tyler
Series Editors: Jane Chisholm and Rosie Dickins
Designed by Mary Cartwright and Brian Voakes
Cover photograph © David H Wells/CORBIS
Illustrations by Gary Cross
Additional illustrations by
Brian Voakes and Andy Burton

This edition produced for:
The Book People Ltd, Hall Wood Avenue,
Haydock, St Helens WA11 9UL

TRUE
ESCAPE
STORIES

Paul Dowswell

CONTENTS

CONTENTS

Breakout at Alcatraz

In the 1930s Alcatraz, a tiny rocky island in San Francisco Bay, was one of the world's most notorious prisons. Known as "The Rock", it was said to be escape proof, and was a bleak home for such notorious gangsters as "Creepy" Karpis and "Machine Gun" Kelly. Al Capone, the most famous gangster of all, traded a life of crime and luxury for the prison's dull routine, and slowly lost his mind working in the laundry room.

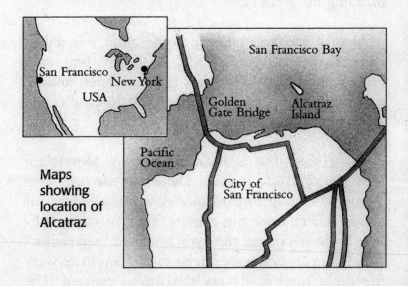

San Francisco Bay

San Francisco New York

USA

Golden Gate Bridge

Alcatraz Island

Pacific Ocean

City of San Francisco

Maps showing location of Alcatraz

By the 1950s, Alcatraz had become a crumbling shadow of its former self. Its villains were no longer notorious, although they were often just as brutal. Now the island was a dumping ground for persistently troublesome prisoners who were transferred there from other jails in the American West.

Frank Morris, bankrobber and burglar, was such a man. A series of prison sentences, escapes and recapture, had led him here. He arrived in January 1960, refusing to accept that "The Rock" was escape proof. From his first moments on the island he was planning his getaway.

Morris was a gaunt, handsome man, not unlike Clint Eastwood, who would later play him in a Hollywood film. His pleasant face and quiet, amiable manner disguised a ruthless determination and razor-sharp mind.

As his first days at Alcatraz went by, Morris got used to the prison routine. There was the daily visit to the workshop to earn money making brushes or gloves. There were the routine body searches, half-hourly head counts, the two hours of "recreation" wandering around the exercise yard. Then there were the three meals a day in the prison canteen. The canteen was considered to be one of the most dangerous places in the prison. As a precaution against an outbreak of rioting, ominous rifle slits had been built into the walls, and silver tear-gas bombs nestled in the ceiling.

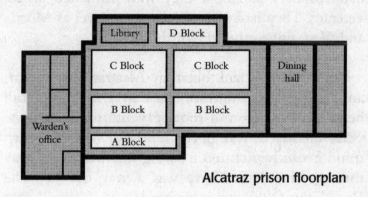

Alcatraz prison floorplan

After the evening meal, the prisoners were locked in their cells for the night. They had four hours to themselves before lights-out at 9:00pm. Here they could paint, read, play musical instruments or whatever, all in the relative privacy of their cells. Some called out chess moves to opponents nearby, others swapped jibes and threats with prisoners they planned to attack during an afternoon exercise period.

Morris's easy manner soon made him friends. In the cell next to him was Allen West, an accordion-playing New York car thief. The two men got along well. In the canteen, where the prisoners could sit where they liked at meal times on long tables and benches, Morris also met the Anglin brothers, John and Clarence. They were burly country boys, who left behind a life as Florida farm hands for a career in bank robbery, and now they were hardened prison veterans. They had cells on the same level as Morris and West, but further down the row.

After Morris had been in Alcatraz for a year, another prisoner told him that a large fan motor had been removed from a rooftop ventilator shaft three years before. It was never replaced. Morris's sharp mind instantly pictured a daring night-time getaway through the shaft. There was a way out of "The Rock" 9m (30ft) above his head.

An escape would be difficult but not impossible. One thing was certain – it would take a great deal of time and planning. But time is the only luxury a man has during his term of imprisonment, and Morris was going to make the best of it.

The first thing Morris had to do was figure out a way of getting from a locked cell up to the roof. The men were watched closely during the time they were out of their cells, so going up there then would be impossible. But one day, inspiration struck. At the bottom of every cell, just below the sink, sat a small air vent. Behind it lay a narrow corridor carrying water, electricity and sewer pipes. If Morris could remove the vent and then make a hole big enough for him to crawl through, he would be able to climb up to the ventilator shaft and out on to the roof. At night he was left alone in his cell for a whole nine hours. This would be a perfect time to explore.

Prison cell floorplan

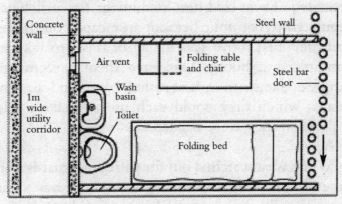

How easy would it be to make that hole? Morris stooped down and picked at the concrete around the vent with a pair of steel nail clippers. Tiny flakes fell away. The concrete could be dug out but it would take ages to do it. And making the hole wasn't the only problem. Hiding it as it got bigger was also a major consideration.

Morris decided he could order an accordion, like West's, to hide his early excavations, paying for it with money he had earned from the prison workshop. As the hole grew slowly bigger and became too big to conceal with the accordion, Morris also hit on the idea of making a false wall with a painted board, complete with a painted-on air vent.

The more Morris plotted, the more he realized an escape like this would be better made with others to help him. West and the Anglin brothers were quickly recruited. Their closeness to him in the cell block would help. The four became an escape committee, and their first move was for all of them to take up painting as a hobby. This gave them a seemingly innocent excuse to order brushes, paints and drawing boards which they could each use to make a false wall when they were needed.

While West watched out for patrolling guards from his cell next door, Morris began to chip away at the concrete with his clippers. After a slow hour he had collected a small pile of fragments, and his fingers ached terribly.

He grumbled quietly to West: "I reckon at this rate we'll still be digging by the time we come up for parole."

"We'll have to have ourselves a little talk with the Anglins at breakfast," said West, and the two retired to their bunks to sleep.

"Weeeellll. . ."

Clarence Anglin always left a word hanging in the air, but what he said afterwards was almost always worth waiting for. West and Morris hung on to his every word.

"See this spoon? I reckon we can make ourselves a proper digging tool with this. You stick your clippers to that handle, and you get a lot more digging done."

Morris slipped his spoon into his pocket.

"Great idea, Clarence," he said. "And I know just how to put spoon and blade together! Catch you later. . ."

That night, as other men painted, or played their instruments, Morris prepared his cell for some ingenious improvised metal work. First he broke the handle off his stolen spoon, and then removed one of the blades from his nail clippers.

"Hey Westy," he whispered, "You got a dime?"

"Yeah, who's asking?"

"Gimme it, I'll pay you back when we break out of here! Now keep a look out for me."

Morris began to chip off tiny slivers of silver from the dime until he had made a little pile on his table. Then he tied fifty or so matches into a tight bundle. Next he piled some books into two close towers and positioned the spoon handle and clipper blade in the gap between the books so that they were touching.

Finally he carefully sprinkled the silver slivers on top of the spoon and blade.

"Anyone coming? Good. Here goes!"

WHOOOOOOSH. Morris ignited the bundle of matches beneath the handle and blade and, for a brief second or two, they were bathed in a fierce white heat, which quickly settled into a fast burning orange flame.

"Bingo!" he cried quietly to himself. Sure enough the heat had melted the silver, and fused the handle and blade together.

"What's that smell Frank? You raising the devil in there?" said West, who caught a strong whiff of burning matches.

Morris checked to see that no guard was approaching then quickly passed his new tool through the bars and into West's cell.

"No kidding," said West. "I'm gonna get me one of these!"

Soon, all four men had made themselves similar digging tools, but they still found hacking away at the concrete was hard, tedious work. After all it was 20cm (8in) thick.

"There's got to be a better way than this," thought Morris, and sure enough, there was.

Allen West enjoyed his job as a prison cleaner. He could wander around chatting with people, and still appear to be working at the same time. The job also brought him several unexpected perks, such as access to electrical equipment. Talking to Morris about the problem of digging through the concrete, he said:

"What we need is the inside of a vacuum cleaner, and I know just where to find one. Take the motor out for the fan, stick in a drill bit on that pivot that goes round, and what have you got – a power drill!!"

"You get me a vacuum motor, and I'll get you a drill bit," said Morris.

West smuggled a motor into his cell, and Morris fitted it up with a drill bit he had stolen from the prison workshop. They both knew it would be terribly noisy so they had to wait until the prison music hour, when the men were allowed to play their instruments in the cells, before they could try it out.

Morris placed the motor's plug into the light socket in his cell.

"Well, here goes. . ."

He flicked the switch and the motor whirred into life. That was loud enough, but the noise it made when the bit hit the concrete was excruciating. Morris drilled for as long as he dared and then stopped. The results were promising. Two holes had gone right through to the other side. Working around these with the blade would be a lot quicker.

Next morning at breakfast Morris filled in the Anglins.

"We'll pass this drill around between the four of us, but we need to use it real careful," he said. "Just make a series of holes when you can, when everyone's blowing, scraping, strumming and honking. This is gonna save us months of digging. Once we got the holes in the wall, digging the rest out with the blades at night will be a walk in the park."

Clarence's eyes lit up. His fingers were completely covered with blisters.

With the escape now looking increasing likely, the men turned their thoughts to getting off the island. Sitting together at the evening meal, they pondered the problems that faced them.

"Water's freezing cold. You got fog almost all year round. Wouldn't like to go to all the trouble of escaping just to freeze to death in that water," said Clarence between mouthfuls.

"The swim's been done," said West. "I heard three girls did it back in '33."

Morris was more realistic: "But they were athletes. They trained for months, they probably covered themselves with goose grease to keep warm, and they definitely weren't living on no prison diet to strengthen them up for the swim. . . and I'll bet they had a support boat follow them over. What we need is a little assistance, a raft, life jacket, something to keep us afloat, or even better, out of that water."

John Anglin spoke next. "I seen a whole pile of plastic raincoats just lying by the workshop. We could steal some of them, take the sleeves off and blow them up like water wings. We could even stick them on any stray planks by the water's edge and make ourselves a raft."

Morris smiled broadly. "As soon as we've got behind that wall, we can start collecting things."

The holes in the wall were getting bigger every day, so the four hurried to complete the false walls that would cover up their handiwork. They painted drawing boards the same shade as the cell wall, and then painted on an air vent. Then they carefully chipped away the wall just around the vent, so that their false wall would fit over it without jutting out.

In bright light the fake walls would not survive a second look, but in the dim recess of a cell they blended in well enough. Now they could dig with less fear of discovery, and soon they had made holes which were big enough to squeeze through.

Getting out at night presented a major problem. All the doors on the cells at Alcatraz were made of steel bars – this meant a patrolling guard could look in to any cells at any time of day to check on the convict within. But Morris had come up with a brilliant solution. Torn pages from magazines were soaked in his cell sink. Then the soggy paper was mashed into a pulp to make papier-mâché, and fashioned into the shape of a head.

After a week or so the head was dry enough to paint. Clarence Anglin, who worked as a prison barber, smuggled Morris some hair the same shade as his, which added a final authentic touch. Morris used the hair to add eyebrows too. Poking out of a blanket at the top of a bunk, in a darkened cell the head would look just like a real one. Rolled up bedding and clothes would make a body shape under the blankets. The prototype head completed, Allen and the Anglins set about making their own dummy heads.

Finally, the night had come to take a trip to the roof. Morris spent the day beforehand trying to curb his restlessness. What if the way up to the roof was blocked? What if the ventilator motor had been replaced after all? All their painstaking work would be wasted. The 12 year sentence stretched out before him. Then another awful thought occurred. The holes in the wall would be discovered eventually, and that would mean even more years added on to his sentence.

At last night fell, and activity in the prison slowly ground to a halt. As West kept an eye out for the guard, Morris placed the dummy head on his pillow and wriggled through the hole at the back of his cell, carefully replacing the false wall behind him.

The corridor behind the wall was a grim, damp place, which stank of the sea water that flowed through its sewage pipes. All around him were ducts and cables, and dust and dirt had settled on everything he touched. But standing up in the tiny corridor Morris felt a huge gleeful rush, like a naughty boy doing something a hated teacher had expressly forbidden.

He had to wait a while for his eyes to become accustomed to the gloom, then he began to make his way up, climbing through a tangle of conduits, mesh, wiring and catwalks to reach the roof ventilator shaft. It stood before him, hanging down 1.5m (5ft) from the roof, and took a sharp right angle 30cm (1ft) inside.

The first thing he realized was that he would need someone else to help lift him inside, and he congratulated himself on having the forethought to realize that escaping as a team would be better than going it alone. Morris also noted that there was plenty of space up here. In this rarely visited and unguarded area of the prison, it would be a perfect place to store material for their long swim to the mainland, a mile or so away.

The next night, Morris and Clarence Anglin made a trip to the roof together. Clarence lifted him inside, but what Morris saw there came like a punch to the stomach. The fan blade and motor had been removed all right, but they had been replaced by two iron bars, a grille and a rain hood. All of these unexpected barriers were firmly anchored in place by solid steel rivets.

They shared the news next morning with West.

"What did you expect to find up there?" he chided, "A couple of airline tickets to Brazil? We got through eight inches of that concrete, so a few bolts ain't gonna stop us now."

West was right. Morris chewed over the problem for a couple of days and came up with a solution. The two bars could be bent back with a length of pipe a repairman had carelessly left in the back corridor. The rivets that held the grille and rain hood in place were far more of a problem. The vacuum cleaner drill would have been handy, but it would make far too much noise. What they needed was something to cut through the rivets. The workshop had a supply of carborundum string – a thin cord coated with abrasive powder, used to saw through metal. It would take many more hours of painstaking work, but it could be done.

So, most nights, a couple of the escapers would climb up to the roof and saw and saw. It was tedious, painful work, but eventually the rivets came away. Morris thought up the clever idea of replacing them with rivet-shaped balls of soap, which they painted black. He did not want a patrolling guard to peer into the shaft and notice the rivets were missing.

Now it was midsummer, 1962. Everything was in place, and there would be no better time of year for an escape. The coldness of the water around the prison made it lethal at most other times of the year. Hunched together in the canteen they haggled about when they should go.

"I say now, and John's with me," said Clarence Anglin. "We've got a huge pile of raincoats waiting to be discovered up in the roof, and those holes in the cells ain't gonna stay secret forever."

"That's true enough," said West. "My fake wall keeps slipping too when I'm outta there at night. I'm gonna have to fix it in there with cement, so let's set a date that will give me time to chip it all out again."

"We'll go in ten or so days," said Morris. "I'm gonna pay a visit to the library, and get me a book on tides. Water in the Bay's dangerous, so we've got to go at a good time, otherwise we'll end up dead."

But over the next week things were getting even more worrying. Convicts would return to their cells after mealtimes and notice small differences – a towel moved here, a book moved there – that gave away the fact that their cell had been searched. Maybe it was just routine checks, or maybe the prison authorities suspected that an escape was coming.

Three days after their last conversation with West, the Anglins could wait no longer. About 9:00pm on the evening of June 11th, Morris heard a voice behind his wall. It was John Anglin telling him that he and Clarence were going NOW. Before Morris could argue, John had headed back up the corridor. Next door, West was panic-stricken. Unprepared, and choking with anger and frustration, he began chipping at the hardened cement seal he had placed around his fake wall.

Morris kept watch for him as long as he could. It was just before lights-out, and the prisoners had yet to settle down for the night. For now, the dull bustle of conversation and activity drowned out West's frantic digging, but Morris could not stay watching out for him much longer.

When the lights were turned off for the night, Morris had to go. He left West digging away, and headed up to the roof. The Anglins were already up there waiting for him. There was no point arguing with them about what they had done to West, they just had to get on and see the escape through without him.

John lifted Morris up to the shaft and he quickly removed the soap rivet heads, his face starkly lit by the recurrent flash of the lighthouse beacon as it swept over the roof. Morris gently eased the grill from its moorings and onto the floor of the roof. But as he lifted away the rainhood, it caught in a sudden gust of wind, and clattered noisily to the floor. Inside the vent, Morris froze. He was so tense he could hardly move.

The three men waited, stock-still in the dark, expecting to hear alarm bells or shouts, and guards rushing up to investigate. Down below, a patrolling guard had indeed heard the noise, and hurried off to tell the duty officer.

"Don't worry about it," he was told. "There's lots of garbage on the roof. It's probably an old paint can blowing around in the wind."

Ten minutes passed before Morris and the Anglins thought it would be safe to move. Each man slowly slithered out onto the roof, with three or four raincoat sleeves tucked around their belts. They all blinked in the harsh glare of the lighthouse beacon. Away from the stuffy hothouse of the prison, the night air felt cool, and the salty sea breeze caught in their nostrils.

The route from rooftop to shore passed through brightly floodlit areas, overlooked by gun towers. There was a lot to do before they could get safely away. The three hugged the shadows as best they could and crawled to the edge of the roof. Morris hauled himself over the rim of the parapet and on to a pipe. Below was a 15m (50ft) drop, and he moved with infinite slowness, lest any sudden movement catch the eye of a guntower guard. He slid down the pipe with the same slow care, and waited for the Anglins to follow.

Away from the cell block the three men carefully made their way over a couple of fences and down a shallow cliff to the seashore. Across the water, the mainland beckoned, just a 2.5km (1.5 mile) swim away.

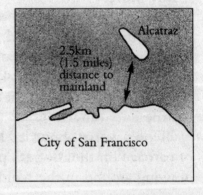

2.5km (1.5 miles) distance to mainland

Alcatraz

City of San Francisco

Crouching in the damp sand, and shivering in the sharp sea breeze, they blew into their raincoat water wings, then waded into the freezing waters of San Francisco Bay. . .

West finally chipped away his false wall after midnight. He hurried up to the roof but Morris and the Anglins were long gone. Poking his head through the ventilator he disturbed a flock of seagulls. They made such a screeching he fled back to his cell in panic. He spent the rest of his sentence wondering what would have happened if the Anglins had given him fair warning of the escape. Maybe he'd be in a quiet backwater bar, with a long cool drink and a beautiful girl. Maybe he'd be lying at the bottom of San Francisco Bay, his bleached bones picked clean by crabs.

After the escape

At daybreak guards sent to rouse the missing men found only dummy heads in their empty beds. Other prison officers recalled the noise that roused their suspicions the night before, and estimated that the men must have entered the water at around 10:00pm that night. It was a good time to go. The Bay was calm, the currents were just right. If the escapers had survived the cold, they had every chance of reaching the mainland.

Boats, soldiers and guards with dogs were all sent out to find them. After two days all they had turned up was a plastic bag full of family photographs belonging to Clarence Anglin.

After that, nothing. No bodies. No clothing. No sightings. The three could have been washed out to sea and drowned, but it is equally likely they escaped. They may even be still alive today.

The getaway from "escape proof" Alcatraz soon became national news, and a severe embarrassment to the prison authorities. The chief guard Olin Blackwell had to admit that the concrete structure of the prison was indeed crumbling away, and this had allowed the prisoners to dig out from their cells.

At the time of the escape many government officials felt that the prison had outlived its usefulness, so in 1963 all the inmates were shipped off the island and dispersed throughout the American penal system.

In 1979 Clint Eastwood starred as Frank Morris in the film *Escape from Alcatraz,* which was made mostly on the island. The film production company spent $500,000 reconnecting electricity and redecorating the prison, which had been closed for 16 years. Most of the actors working on the film became ill in the musty interior of the prison, which gave their performances a realistic convict lethargy. The film brought the escape of Morris and the Anglins to a global audience, and today Alcatraz is a popular tourist attraction.

Relatives of the Anglins say they have received postcards from South America from the brothers, but have never produced them to prove this. Morris, who had no close family, has vanished without trace. Allen West never regained his freedom. He died in a Florida prison in 1978.

Alias Ivan Bagerov

"Getting out of here is going to be a piece of cake. It's getting away that's going to be the most difficult part."

British Royal Navy Lieutenant David James was explaining his escape plan to a fellow prisoner, Captain David Wells. Both were residents of Marlag und Milag Nord Prisoner of War Camp, near Bremen, Germany. It was early winter in 1943, four years into the Second World War.

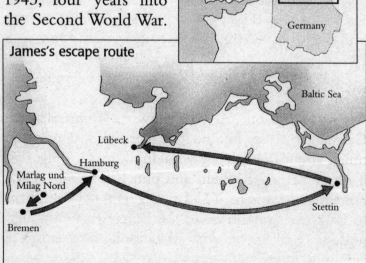

James's escape route

James had concocted two ingenious disguises for himself, to get him from the camp to nearby Sweden, where he would be able to return to Britain.

The two men were sitting in front of a coal fire. Their hut was sparse, but the fire kept out the cold. Outside the window, a dreary, freezing rain had been falling all day. The north German winter had settled with a vengeance.

James outlined his escape in more detail.

"This how I see it. . . I'm a foreigner who speaks only a few words of German. So, I'm going to disguise myself as another foreigner. The guards and officials I'm going to meet will see scores of passes and identity papers everyday. They'll know them like the back of their hand, and will be able to spot a fake from 20 paces. So, I'm going for something obscure they won't have seen before. In fact, I'm going as a Bulgarian!"

Wells looked blank, then completely bewildered.

"Why?"

James went on, "As you know, the Bulgarians are Germany's allies, but no one here seems to know much about them. They wouldn't know a Bulgarian if one came up to them and punched them on the nose. Also, I thought, if I adapt my own navy uniform to look like I might be in the Bulgarian Navy, then no one will know what that looks like either. I certainly don't."

Wells laughed.

"Bulgarian navy! They've only got about three ships. You're on a winning streak there, old chap. What have you got?"

James showed him his props. A friend in the camp, who had been a tailor before the war, had made him a gold and blue shoulder insignia with the letters KBVMF, which stood for Royal Bulgarian Navy.

"Those letters look jolly strange. They're Russian aren't they?" said Wells.

"No, Bulgarian," said James. "They use the same alphabet as the Russians. In fact, that's part of the next step in my plan. I've had a whole bunch of documents forged by a chap over in hut D. He used to work as a book illustrator, and he's done a brilliant job. Look at this!"

James went to his locker and took out a folder full of papers, letters, passes and a big photograph.

"Here's my identity card. Lieutenant Ivan Bagerov – Royal Bulgarian Navy. All that Bulgarian writing won't mean a thing to your average guard."

Wells laughed.

"Who's that handsome chap in the identity card photo? It's certainly not YOU!"

James smiled.

"Well spotted. We found him in a German magazine. He's a German Navy hero. Looks a bit like me, but we put that fake Bulgarian stamp over half his face, so it wouldn't be too obvious it wasn't! I've made sure everything in my case looks Bulgarian, or at least looks like what someone would assume was Bulgarian. I even scraped the manufacturer's stamp off my English soap and etched in a Bulgarian letter."

"Who's that in the big photo?" said Wells. "It looks like that ballet dancer. What's her name?"

James laughed again.

"THAT is Margot Fonteyn. Lovely isn't she! I'm going to tell anyone searching my case she's my Bulgarian fiancée. It should prove to be quite a nice distraction. You know Roberts over in Hut E? He speaks Russian, so I got him to write me a love letter too. We're covering all the angles here! And . . . I've even changed the English labels on my clothes. I couldn't get Bulgarian or Russian labels, but a couple of Greek fellows in the camp have given me some of theirs. They look sufficiently different. And, on top of everything, Bulgaria is also a monarchy, so the crown on my Royal Navy jacket buttons won't look out of place either."

"And then there's THIS!"

James took out another forged document.

"It's a letter of introduction from The Royal Bulgarian Navy. It's written in German and I'm going to show it to anyone who bothers me, or who I think I can get to help me. It says: 'Lieutenant Bagerov is engaged in liaison duties of a technical nature which involve him in much travel. Since he speaks very little German, the usual benevolent assistance of all German officials is confidently solicited on his behalf.' "

Wells laughed at the daring plan. He was certainly impressed. But then he looked worried.

"Uh-oh," he said. "Bad news, James. Quite a few of our Navy chaps here have been into Bremen over the last few weeks to visit the hospital. Your Navy uniform might be a bit different, but it's not different enough. I'm sure someone will recognize it, and have you nabbed."

"I've thought of that too. I'm going to start my escape in another disguise! I've got some silk patches to put over my jacket brass buttons, and a cloth cap made from a jacket lining, and a scarf and a pair of old canvas trousers. I'm going to become Christof Lindholm – Danish electrician! I've got a pass for that too."

"Crikey, you've been busy!" said Wells. "So what happens when you get to Sweden, or even Britain, and you need to prove who you really are?"

"I've got that sorted out too. I've sewn my real identity papers into my jacket lining, so I can go back to being me when I need to."

"Well, best of luck – though with all that lot I don't think you'll need it." said Wells.

James looked a little ill at ease.

"Frankly, old chap, sitting in front of this lovely fire, with the rain coming down outside, I'm not sure I want to escape at all. But so many people have helped me with this scheme I feel I've got to give it a go."

And give it a go he did. On the morning of December 8th, 1943, James made his way down to the shower block on the edge of the camp. Amazingly, a window there opened onto the street outside, so all James had to do was change into his Danish electrician outfit, and squeeze out when he was sure no one was coming.

Walking away in his disguise he could have been any local workman. But trouble loomed almost as soon as he left the camp. He was stopped by a policeman who immediately became suspicious. Inside, James began to panic. All that work and here he was, barely a minute away from the camp, and about to be caught red-handed. The policeman looked in his case. Fortunately it just contained some clothes. James had carefully hidden all Ivan Bagerov's documents – they were strapped to his leg with adhesive bandages.

The policeman began to question him in a hostile way. What was he doing? Who was he? Who was he staying with? It was a nightmare moment. James only spoke a few words of German but blurted out that he was staying with the local priest. He did not even know his name, so just referred to him as "Father".

The policeman was still suspicious. What did the priest look like? James made a wild guess. He was an old man with grey hair, he said, which fortunately turned out to be true. He stumbled on with more of his story, hoping that the policeman didn't start to wonder why this supposed Danish workman had such an odd accent.

The story was not working. The policeman told him to come with him to the police station. But James had another trick up his sleeve – a forged letter from a local hospital, telling him to report there that afternoon. This final detail convinced the policeman that James was the Danish electrician he was pretending to be. The man dismissed him with a curt "Good day" and James hurried off, feeling quite sick and doing his best to stop his legs from trembling as he walked.

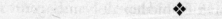

James reached Bremen station without further trouble, and headed at once for the platform lavatory. There, the cap and canvas trousers of his electrician's outfit were hidden behind a cistern. Away from the middle of the town, James felt it was now safe to take on his Bulgarian disguise. Inside the tiny w.c. cubicle he removed the silk patches from his buttons, sewed on the shoulder insignia, and darkened his light hair with theatrical make up, to make him look more Eastern European.

Christof Lindholm had disappeared – and out stepped Ivan Bagerov. Taking a deep breath to steady his nerves, James walked up to a station guard, and presented him with his forged letter of introduction.

The man read the letter and gave James a smile.

"Where are you going to, sir?" he said.

James told him he was heading for the port of Lübeck, on the Baltic Sea. This would be the perfect spot to head for Sweden.

"Follow me, sir," said the guard briskly, and they walked off to the ticket office.

James's letter worked like a magic charm. The guard found out which trains he would have to take, wrote down the details for him, and gave him a ticket. Then he took him to the station waiting room and bought him a beer from the bar! James had to struggle to stop himself from laughing out loud, or gushing with gratitude. He wanted to give the man a big hug, but forced himself to remain as aloof and formal as he thought a visiting Bulgarian naval officer ought to be.

The train arrived, and James was soon heading for the coast. The officials he met on his way – ticket inspectors, policemen, guards – all stared blankly at his Bulgarian pass, and all of them waved him on his way with a polite nod.

After a couple of hours the train pulled into Hamburg, where James needed to change trains. He had to spend an hour in the waiting room, and here he was stared at suspiciously by a German soldier. James was sure this man had seen through his disguise and recognized his Royal Navy uniform, but he decided to bluff it out. He thought "What would I do if I was really Ivan Bagerov and someone was staring at me? Why, stare straight back!"

James glared at the man with such hostility the soldier became embarrassed and let his gaze slip to the floor. He left the waiting room shortly afterwards. James wondered if he had gone to fetch a policeman, but by the time the train arrived no one had bothered him.

The journey passed slowly. James had to get off the train again to spend an uncomfortable night in a waiting room in Bad Kleinen, but he had covered 320km (200 miles) in a single day. His escape was going better than he could ever have imagined.

The next day the train continued on to Stettin, another port on the Baltic Sea. James thought he would try his luck here, as Stettin was just as likely to have Swedish ships as Lübeck.

But it didn't. As James wandered along the waterfront there was not a single Swedish ship to be seen. Cursing his luck he headed into the town, and went to several bars, hoping to overhear some Swedish voices.

By late afternoon James realized Stettin had been a big mistake. There was nothing else to do but continue on his journey. So he returned to the station and caught a train heading to Lübeck. Again, he had to get off the train in the evening, and spent another uncomfortable night in the dining room of a very crowded military rest camp. As James tried to sleep at a table in the corner of the room, he was joined by several German Naval officers. He couldn't have wished for worse companions, and felt sure they would recognize his British uniform. But they must have been even more tired than he was, for they said nothing to him, nor even gave him a second glance.

Next day he hurried off to the station and arrived in Lübeck by late morning. By now his smart lieutenant image was beginning to look a bit shabby, especially as he had two days of stubble on his chin. James headed for the nearest barber and asked, in halting German, if he could have a shave. The barber looked at him in astonishment.

"Don't you know?" the man said rather rudely. "Don't you know about the soap ration? No one has had a shave at a barbers for two years!"

James gave an embarrassed shrug, and fled from the shop in a near panic, certain that everyone in the street was looking at him.

Feeling flustered, he booked himself into a hotel, where he left his suitcase, and headed for the docks. Here things looked up. The first thing he saw on the quayside were two Swedish ships. But between him and them were guarded dock gates.

A guard stood at one side of the road, so James followed a large truck which was going into the docks, taking care that he stayed on the other side of it from the guard. Once on the quayside he walked up the gangplank of the nearest Swedish ship, and headed for the crew quarters. The ship was taking on a cargo of coal, and coal dust hung in the chilly winter air, making him cough.

James could hear Swedish voices coming from a cabin, and knocked on the steel door. He walked in and saw two men sitting at a table sipping coffee. They looked up expectantly. Then one of them smiled and spoke to him in excellent English.

"Royal Navy, I believe. I'd recognize your uniform a mile away!"

James laughed. He was relieved that the man was so friendly.

"Yes," said James. "It's not much of a disguise. I'm actually supposed to be Ivan Bagerov of the Royal Bulgarian Navy!"

The men invited James to share a cup of coffee with them, and he told them his story, and asked if they would take him to Sweden.

The man who spoke English gave a sorry shrug.

"Look my friend, I'd love to help, but it can't be done. When this coal is loaded into the hold, we've got several German dock hands coming on board to refuel the ship. They're bound to see you on board, and if they suspect you're a stowaway, then we'll all be arrested. You can see for yourself that the ship's just too small for there to be anywhere to hide you."

James was crestfallen. The man had been so friendly he felt sure he would help him. He had even begun to think his ordeal was almost over.

"Please," he begged. "I've been on the run for three days now, and this is the first time I've felt safe. There must be somewhere I can hide?"

But the Swede had made up his mind. He spoke firmly, in a tone that made it plain that there was nothing more to discuss.

"I'd like to help you, but I certainly don't want to end up in a concentration camp. Look over there," he said, pointing out of the cabin porthole. "That ship is heading for Sweden, too. It's leaving any minute, so try your luck there."

That was that. James thanked the man and got up to leave. Standing on the deck, he surveyed the route down the gangplank and onto the other ship. Having felt so safe and near to success mere minutes ago, the trip between this ship and the next seemed terribly dangerous, and a huge unreachable distance. James's nerve was finally going.

As he walked down the plank, he saw to his horror that the other ship was about to leave the quayside. James ran, but he was too late. For one crazy moment he thought he could just leap on board, but he was sure he would be spotted and the boat would be stopped before it left German waters.

"Right," he said to himself, "back to the hotel, and try again tomorrow." But now, dispirited and exhausted, James became careless. He did not bother to hide from the guard at the entrance of the dock, and he was spotted and stopped. Perhaps his unshaven appearance gave him away, for this time the Ivan Bagerov story did not work. The guard insisted that James go with him to the local police station to have his papers checked more thoroughly.

There was nothing James could do but go. Besides, he was not too worried. There was still a chance that the police would be as baffled as everyone else had been by his Bulgarian documents.

Shortly afterwards, James stood in front of the desk of a senior officer at Lübeck police station. The man examined his identity card with a magnifying glass and said quite casually in English:
"So, where did you escape from?"
James, who had been holding his breath in anticipation, let out a long sigh. Actually, he felt quite relieved that it was all over.

The policeman was surprisingly polite. He offered James a seat and called in several of his colleagues. One of them mocked the forged pass, but another congratulated James on such a good forgery, especially as he had had such limited resources in his prison camp. He even told James that he should have put Polizei Präsident on the pass, instead of Polizei Kommissar.

Everyone seemed quite amused by his tale, which made James feel more at ease. After all, he had heard that escapers were sometimes shot if they were caught. The man who escorted him back to the local military jail even told him he was sorry he had had such bad luck.

After the escape

James was sent back to Marlag und Milag Nord and spent ten days in solitary confinement in a punishment cell. His desire to escape had not left him. Five weeks later he was gone again, this time disguised as a merchant seaman. Taking the same route, he successfully boarded a ship to Sweden. This time he got there, and was able to make his way safely back to England.

Once home, James wrote *An Escaper's Progress*, an account of his adventures in Marlag und Milag Nord. He noted that being an escaper is like meeting someone at a party whose name you cannot remember. You have to pick up clues as you talk, by asking leading questions. In this way he learned how to get by without drawing attention to himself in the places and situations he found himself in.

After the war James became an Antarctic explorer, and was a Conservative Member of Parliament between 1959–1964 and 1970–1979. He also helped to set up the Loch Ness Investigation Bureau, an organization dedicated to finding evidence of the Loch Ness Monster.

A spy in the Scrubs

Night fell early on Saturday October 22nd, 1966. An overcast sky and chilly north wind reminded visitors to London's Hammersmith Hospital that winter would soon be upon them. Along the side of the hospital was a small alleyway, which separated it from Wormwood Scrubs prison. Parked in the alley, in a nondescript blue saloon car, sat a sullen, anxious-looking man, who cradled a bunch of chrysanthemums.

Anybody who fleetingly noticed him would assume he was planning to visit a relative in the hospital. But a longer glance would have revealed that he was talking to his chrysanthemums in a rather agitated, impatient way. The man was Sean Bourke, and what he was actually doing was speaking into a walkie-talkie hidden in the flowers. He was about to commit an exceptionally serious crime.

Wormwood Scrubs was a dreary Victorian building. It was home to many of London's petty criminals. Most had been given short sentences, and none were considered particularly dangerous, apart from one. Among the burglars, car thieves and sellers of stolen goods, was the infamous spy George Blake. A former senior officer in MI6 (the British secret service), Blake had betrayed at least 42 British agents to the communist Soviet Union, and passed on other vital top secret information to Britain's enemies.

His trial in 1961 had caused a sensation, and he had been sentenced to 42 years in prison, the longest term ever given to a spy in peacetime. Blake had been placed in Wormwood Scrubs, in West London, because the British secret service needed to talk to him from time to time. They were based in London, and it would be convenient to have him reasonably nearby.

With hindsight this was not a smart move. Blake was a very clever man, with a fascinating, tangled history. Born Georg Behar in Holland, of a Dutch mother and Jewish father, his loyalty lay with his communist beliefs, rather than any one country. He fought with the Dutch resistance when the country was occupied by the Nazis in 1940, then escaped to Britain in 1943. He joined the Royal Navy, where he was recruited into the British secret service. Caught up in the Korean War, he survived three years as a prisoner of the North Koreans. On his return he had become convinced communism was the best system of government, and gave top secret information to the Soviet Union, the world's leading communist nation, for almost ten years.

Curiously, Blake was a popular prisoner in "the Scrubs". A tall, charming man, he taught illiterate prisoners to read and write, and was courteous and cooperative with the prison guards. Some prisoners sympathized with his communist views, and others felt his sentence was too harsh. He had made many friends in prison. Among them were Sean Bourke, a small-time villain, and Pat Pottle and Michael Randle – two peace activists jailed for their part in a demonstration at an American airbase in Britain. All three had recently been released from prison, and had decided to help him escape.

Now, as Bourke fidgeted outside in the gloom, Blake was standing in the bright glare of Hall D, chatting with one of the prison officers about whether television wrestling matches were faked. The guard was so engrossed in the conversation he failed to notice another prisoner, a friend of Blake's, carefully removing two panes of glass from a large window above his head.

The conversation over, Blake headed back to his cell, picked up a walkie-talkie radio recently smuggled into the prison, and made his way to the broken window. The hall was now virtually empty, as most guards and prisoners were at the weekly movie, which was shown every Saturday evening.

Unseen, he slipped out into the cold night air and leaped down to a porch roof below the window. From there he jumped onto a waste container and then down to the ground. Before him stood a 6m (20ft) high brick wall.

"Sean, Sean, can you hear me?" he whispered into his walkie-talkie, as he crouched in the shadows.

But there was no reply. Bourke was busy. Two young lovers were kissing and cuddling in a car parked all too close to his own. Naturally, he did not want any witnesses to this escape. Pretending to be a prison official, he was busy trying to shoo the couple away.

Blake waited for what seemed like an eternity, his heart pounding in his chest and a terrible fear lurking in his stomach. The missing window panes would be spotted all too soon, and he had only a few minutes to get away. Blake had been in Wormwood Scrubs for four weary years, and the visits by the secret service men were becoming more and more infrequent. He knew they would soon transfer him to a top security prison outside London, where escape would be all but impossible. This was going to be his one and only chance to get away.

Eventually Blake's radio crackled.

"George? Are you there? Thank Heavens! Look, I'm throwing the ladder over now."

Another terrible, still silence ensued. Then came a clattering sound as a lightweight ladder, made from washing line and knitting needles, snaked over the wall.

"OK Sean, hold tight, I'm coming over now," whispered Blake, and he ran from the shadows and out to the ladder, certain he would be spotted at any second.

He climbed clumsily, scraping his fingers on the rough brickwork. Blake was not an athletic man, and this physical exercise quickly tired him. Standing on top of the wall, panting and puffing, he looked down to see Bourke and his car. Freedom was only seconds away, but Blake was so desperate to escape, he could not even wait that long. Rather than climbing down the outer wall he leaped from the top, breaking a wrist and cutting his face as he landed.

"Good Heavens, man," said Bourke, "are you all right? There was no need to do that!"

He picked up his friend and bundled him into the back of his car. Then he dashed around to the driver's seat and started the engine. The car spluttered into life, and Bourke shot off up the alley, scattering hospital visitors and crashing into the back of a car in front of him. Before the outraged driver could get out, Bourke had clumsily lurched around him, and driven off to merge into the stream of early evening traffic heading away from central London.

"We did it! We did it!" he shouted jubilantly.

In the back seat, Blake was holding his broken wrist and wincing with every bump in the road. But despite this, and the blood dripping down his face, he was grinning like a madman.

All the dull indignities of prison life flashed before him – the miserable, stale floorcloth stench of the place, the taste of limp, lukewarm cabbage, some of the Scrubs' creepier residents. . .

"Good Lord, what I've had to put up with these last four years!" he exclaimed.

Blake was ecstatic. Then, for a second, he looked more serious.

"It's not over yet though is it? I've got this to sort out," he said, holding up his arm, "and then I've got to get out of this country."

"All in good time, George, all in good time," said Bourke. "First we'll get you back to the hiding place I've found for you, and have something decent to eat."

It was only a short journey, and as far as they could tell, no one was following them. Bourke had found

Blake a room in a house, in a seedy, anonymous street not far from the prison. Bourke parked in front of the house. They waited until the street was clear, then walked quickly in before anyone spotted them.

Inside, Bourke bathed the wound on Blake's face, and bandaged up his damaged wrist the best he could. Then he left to go and dump the car a good distance away. He returned with a bottle of whisky and a bottle of brandy.

"This will help us wash down our supper," he laughed. "And wait until you see what I've got to eat!"

Bourke was soon frying two huge steaks. When they were ready he cut Blake's into small pieces and watched as he wolfed it down with one hand. Blake was ravenously hungry, and soon had appalling indigestion.

"Four years of prison food," he laughed, "and now this. No wonder I feel sick!"

"Have some brandy," suggested Bourke, "that'll sort you out!"

After finishing their steaks, Bourke and Blake talked about the escape.

"The trouble we've had getting you out of there," Bourke said.

He told his friend all about how he, Pottle and Randle had tried to contact Blake's family to raise funds for the escape, and how they had fallen out over Bourke's inability to provide receipts for everything he bought.

"I mean, how do you get a receipt for a forged passport?" Bourke snorted.

He told Blake how they had planned everything, from getaway car to radio sets, knitting needle rope to false passports. The whole escape had come to £700, money which the three had put up themselves and borrowed from friends.

In between drinks they ate strawberries and cream. But while they were eating, a television show they were watching was interrupted by a news flash. A serious looking man announced:

"Soviet spy, George Blake, has escaped from Wormwood Scrubs prison, in London. The escape happened at around 6:30pm this evening. Blake climbed over the prison wall using a ladder thrown to him by an accomplice. The two men are believed to have driven off in a small blue car, heading west out of London."

A recent picture of Blake appeared on the screen, a prison mug shot of him looking stern and distant.

"A news flash!" said Bourke. "They didn't even wait for the main bulletin. You're Britain's most wanted man!"

Bourke laughed. But Blake looked more serious.

"I hope no one saw us come into the house," he said. "Every policeman in London will be looking for me."

❖

The next day Bourke went out to find a doctor. Blake knew Bourke had a network of sympathetic friends, but his own background in espionage taught him that no one could really be trusted. Every contact they made like this laid them open to the possibility of betrayal.

Around noon, Bourke returned with a doctor, and a bundle of newspapers. The doctor was a serious young man who greeted Blake coolly, then treated his broken wrist. It was agonizing, and Blake drank the last of Bourke's whiskey to deaden the pain.

After the doctor had gone, Blake said:

"Are you sure he won't betray us? He didn't seem very friendly."

"Don't worry," said Bourke. "He's on our side. He was probably just worried about helping a runaway convict! Now look at this. . ."

Bourke showed Blake the day's papers. They were full of stories of the escape. One paper had made much of the chrysanthemums Bourke had left behind in his hurry to get away. The paper painted a picture of him as a shadowy criminal mastermind, and wrote that his chrysanthemums were a mysterious calling card.

The two men laughed at the way their escape had been presented to the British public. They were particularly amused by one newspaper's theory that a substitute had been sent to prison in his place and allowed to escape, while the real Blake had returned to Moscow as a double agent.

But all this publicity was bad news. Blake's face was on the front page of every newspaper, and flashed on television at every news broadcast. They were going to have to be extremely careful. Although the doctor who treated Blake's wrist never did give them away, they still thought it best to move to a nearby house to stay with a man who was a friend of Randle and Pottle. This proved to be a disaster. The man's wife told her psychiatrist that they were hiding two men from the police, so another bolt hole was needed urgently.

Bourke too had made a silly mistake. Despite all his careful planning for the escape, he had bought the getaway car they used in his own name, and the police had traced it. Now his photograph was appearing alongside Blake's on every newspaper front page, and his name was being mentioned on every radio and television news bulletin.

By early November they had moved to Pat Pottle's house, which was also in London. Tired of all this hiding, Blake was now desperate to leave the country. But, two weeks after the escape, his name and photograph were still all over the papers and television. It would be too risky to try to leave the country in the normal way, via a ferry or plane, even using a false passport.

Pottle and Randle tried to alter Blake's appearance dramatically. They gave him a drug called Meladinin which was supposed to make skin much darker, and also put him under a sun-lamp for several tanning sessions. The experiment was a miserable failure. Blake still looked instantly recognizable. But Randle came to the rescue with another ruse.

He had a large Volkswagen camper van, and Blake was hidden in its blanket compartment. Randle and his family drove to Europe, telling border police they were going sight-seeing in East Germany. At the time, this country was controlled by the Soviet Union so Blake would be safe there.

The trip went without a hitch, and a very stiff and slightly carsick Blake was dropped off just outside Berlin. He introduced himself to the first East German soldier he could find, but no one believed his story. He was taken to Berlin, and a Soviet secret service officer who knew him personally was flown over to see him. When this officer walked in, hugged him and started to shout "It's him! It's him!" Blake knew his troubles were over.

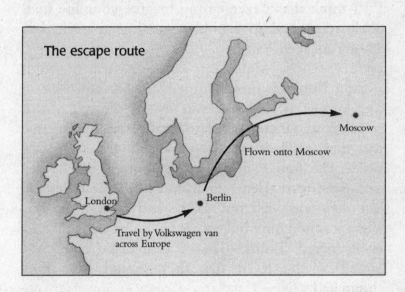

The escape route

Flown onto Moscow

Moscow

London

Berlin

Travel by Volkswagen van
across Europe

After the escape

Blake was handsomely rewarded by his Soviet allies. He was made an colonel in the KGB (the Soviet security service) and put up in a comfortable apartment in Moscow. He had left behind a wife and three sons in England, but remarried a Russian woman and had another daughter. He was found work as a researcher in international politics and economics for Moscow University. Still alive today, he has no regrets about his past. When recently asked if he felt the collapse of communism in the Soviet Union had meant that all his efforts had been wasted, he said:

"I think it is never wrong to give your life to a noble ideal, and to a noble experiment, even if it doesn't succeed."

Sean Bourke's future turned out bleaker. Not as well-known as Blake, he was able to slip out of the country on a false passport. He flew to Berlin, and was then sent on to Moscow and reunited with Blake. The two men got along so well, the Soviet authorities put them up in an apartment together. But they soon fell out. Blake had been charming when it suited him, but he could also be arrogant and ill-mannered. Bourke related that Blake had even hinted to the KGB that they should have him eliminated.

Bourke eventually returned to his native Ireland and wrote a book about the escape called *The Springing of George Blake*. His account disguised the part Pottle and Randle played, to protect them from arrest. The book became a best seller and he turned full time to writing, but with no further success. He became an alcoholic and died alone in a mobile home in Ireland, in 1982.

Pat Pottle and Michael Randle's role in Blake's getaway became public knowledge in 1989, when

British newspapers published sensational accounts of the escape. The two men were prosecuted and brought to trial. Despite the fact that they had clearly broken the law, the jury was sympathetic to them and they were acquitted. Pat Pottle died in 2000, but Michael Randle is still a campaigning writer and journalist, and a research fellow at the Department of Peace Studies at the University of Bradford.

The dirty docker

If the guards at Donington Hall Prisoner of War Camp had known a bit more about Kapitänleutnant Gunther Plüschow, they might have kept a closer eye on him. To the men who watched over him, he was a genial, well-dressed fellow, who spoke very good English. He had a friendly smile, and was good at hockey, which he played at every opportunity. He was really quite charming.

He was also extremely clever and, if he had anything to do with it, he was not going to be staying in Donington Hall for long.

Plüschow's background was exceptional. A cadet at Munich's Military School from the age of 10, he excelled in everything he did. After an outstanding career as a marine in the German Imperial Army, he volunteered to become one of Germany's first airforce pilots. After learning to fly he was sent to Tsingtao in China, which was a German colony. When the First World War broke out in 1914 Tsingtao was attacked by British and Japanese forces, and Plüschow gained a reputation as a daring flyer. While in China, he had had a dragon tattooed to his left arm, and his men took to calling him "The Dragon Master".

When it seemed certain that Tsingtao would fall, Plüschow was ordered to make his way back to Germany. He was captured by Chinese troops, but soon gave them the slip, and took a boat from Shanghai to San Francisco, USA. After making his way to New York, he took a boat to Italy. Unfortunately for him, the boat stopped at Gibraltar – a British port on the Mediterranean. Plüschow was arrested as a prisoner of war, and taken to England.

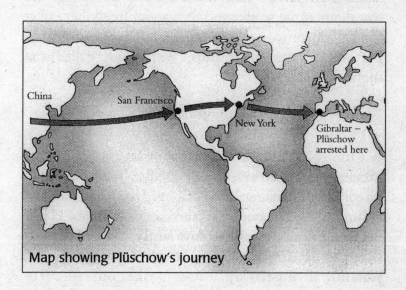

Map showing Plüschow's journey

He was taken to Donington Hall, an old stately home which had been turned into a prison camp.

Life there was actually quite pleasant. Plüschow, who had arrived with all his luggage, was allowed to receive packages and letters from his family, and spent most of his time chatting to other officers and playing sports.

The camp routine was very relaxed. Twice a day there was a parade for a roll call – a register to check on all the inmates. There was also a rule the men had to follow about a day boundary and a night boundary. The day boundary took in much of the grounds of the home, including a pleasant park, and had a high barbed wire fence around it. During the day the men were allowed to wander freely here. But after dark, prisoners were expected to keep within the area around their huts, which was called the night boundary.

One of Plüschow's companions was another officer named Oberleutnant Trefftz. Like Plüschow he spoke excellent English. He also knew the country well, having visited several times. They became friends and Plüschow suggested they escape together. Trefftz agreed and the two men set about planning their getaway.

Both men knew that getting out of the camp would be fairly easy, but what came after would be difficult. Donington was near the town of Derby, which lay a few miles to the north. Here they could catch a train to London, and then stowaway on board a boat heading for Holland – a neutral country where they could make their way to Germany.

Map showing location of Donington

Derby

Donington

London

Plüschow and Trefftz hatched a simple but ingenious plan based on their knowledge of the guards' routine. They also asked their fellow prisoners to help them with their escape and to give them money to buy food and pay for their journey. On July 4th, 1915 the two men claimed to be ill, and the camp doctor placed them on the official sick list. This meant they were excused from the daily roll call parades.

At 4:00pm that afternoon, after a day resting in bed, they both got up and dressed in civilian clothes. Plüschow had brought a stylish suit from China, a blue sweater and a smart gray overcoat. The men were supposed to wear their uniforms at the camp, so they put on their officer's caps and coats as well.

After they dressed, they gobbled down all the buttered rolls that had been left in the hut for the prisoners' afternoon snack. It could be several days before they ate again. Then they prepared to leave. Outside it was raining cats and dogs. Normally they would curse such dull British weather, but as Plüschow pointed out, this was perfect for their escape.

"Trefftz, my dear fellow," he said, "the Gods are on our side. The guards are going to be shivering and dripping wet in their little guard boxes. They're not going to be paying much attention to us!"

"A guard box will be a better place to spend the next four hours than what we're planning to do," said Trefftz, who was not looking forward to being soaked to the bone.

The two men walked out of their hut and into the rain. They ambled rather stiffly in their many layers of clothing, and made their way over to the park. There, near the barbed wire boundary, lay a pile of deck chairs. After a quick glance around to make sure no one was watching them, the two men stooped down and hid among the chairs.

After an hour the rain stopped, and Plüschow and Trefftz shivered and cursed in their cramped hiding place. Both were now feeling quite anxious about their escape attempt, and this tedious wait was making them jumpy.

The camp clock struck six, and the prisoners came out of their huts for the evening roll call.

"Stage one," said Plüschow. "If this fails, expect to see some bad-tempered guards with bayonets on their rifles, poking around in the undergrowth."

The two men peeked out from the chairs, as their fellow prisoners assembled. The ritual of the roll call drifted across the park, each prisoner barking a curt yes as his name was called. Plüschow and Trefftz's names were unanswered of course, but they were reported sick. As soon as the roll call was over, two of their fellow officers rushed back to occupy their beds. The camp guard sent to check that they were there, saw what he thought were two sleeping figures, and assumed it was them.

Plüschow and Trefftz waited, anticipating an alarm or call-out for the guards, which would tell them that their plan had failed. But everything seemed to go on as usual.

After evening roll call, the day boundary was out of bounds, and the guards withdrew to the night boundary. So all Plüschow and Trefftz had to do now was climb over an unguarded barbed wire fence. But there was one more problem with the camp routine which had to be overcome.

A slow summer dusk fell over Donington Hall, and turned to a black moonless night. At bedtime, a guard checked every bed, and once again the escapers' fellow officers would help them. Because all the prisoners were so familiar with the guards routine, they knew the exact order in which each hut would be visited. Two men from a hut the guards always checked first sneaked over to Plüschow and Trefftz's hut and got into their beds.

Again, in their cramped, damp hiding place the two escapers listened out for any clue that their escape had been discovered. But the dull routine of Donington Hall seemed as unchanging as ever.

"So far, so good," said Plüschow, "so let's go!"

"For Heaven's sake don't knock anything over." said Trefftz with a grin. "Any noise and we'll have dogs barking and alarm bells ringing, and we'll be finished."

Like dark shadows the two men rose from the tangle of chairs, and made their way to the wire.

"Watch out for the fourth strand up," said Plüschow. "That one is electric. Touch that and it sets an alarm off in the camp."

"How did you know that?" said Trefftz.

"It pays to eavesdrop!" said Plüschow. "I overheard two of the guards talking about it."

Slowly, slowly, one by one, the two men climbed the wire. If they were careful, and they took care to untangle any bit of clothing that had caught on a barb, it was quite easy to get over. But still, Plüschow made a large rip in his trousers when he jumped the final six feet down to the ground.

Away from the wire, and into a dense forest that stood by the road away from the camp, they buried their uniform coats and caps under drifting leaves and brushwood.

"Now, which way to Derby?" said Trefftz.

But even as he spoke, a soldier loomed out of the dark towards them. Plüschow immediately grabbed Trefftz, hugged him tightly and began to kiss him!

Trefftz was too startled to do anything but go along with this ploy, and when the soldier walked past them hurriedly, tutting with embarrassment, he had to grit his teeth to stop giggling.

The danger passed, Plüschow released his companion with a smirk.

"Unseemly conduct for an officer and a gentleman," said Trefftz primly.

They hurried down the road, wanting to get as far away from the camp and anyone who might recognize them as quickly as possible. An hour or so later, they came to a crossroads.

A sign stood at the corner of the road, but it was so dark they could not see what it said. Plüschow climbed up it and traced the letters with his finger.

"D. . . E. . . R. . . B. . ."

"Derby. Yes, this is it. Let's go!"

They walked all night, spurred on by the knowledge that as soon as their escape was discovered, the station was the first place the police and army would look.

As dawn broke they stopped to tidy themselves up. Plüschow repaired his trousers with a needle and thread he always carried, and both men shaved, using their own spit as shaving foam. Doing this was faintly repulsive, but anything that gave a policeman or soldier any clue that they might be two runaways, rather than a couple of well-dressed fellows, had to be avoided at all costs.

Shortly after, they reached the railway station and bought railway tickets to London. Standing on the near deserted platform with a handful of early morning commuters made Plüschow feel uneasy.

"Look, my friend," he said to Trefftz, "we're too obvious together. Let's split up. I'll see you in London, on the steps of St. Paul's Cathedral, at 7:00pm tonight."

Trefftz could immediately see the sense in Plüschow's suggestion. He gave his friend a wink, then wandered to the other end of the platform.

The train arrived, the two men got on and Plüschow's journey passed in a sleepy haze. Once in London he headed for St. Paul's, but Trefftz did not appear. Plüschow waited an hour, then headed for Hyde Park, where he thought he could hide and sleep.

But the park was closed, and so Plüschow crept into the grounds of a house nearby, and hid in the bushes at the bottom of the garden. Unlike the night before, this summer evening was dry and warm, and Plüschow began to nod off to sleep. Then a noise disturbed him and he came to his senses with a start.

A party was going on in the house, and some of the guests had come out onto the lawn to enjoy the night air. Plüschow froze in the bushes, hardly daring to breathe. A few feet away elegant gentlemen and ladies in long ball gowns swanned around making conversation. Once he got used to it, Plüschow found it all quite funny, and enjoyed listening to the party guests as they traded scandalous gossip, or complained about their servants.

As he began to relax, the sound of a piano and a woman singing a beautiful song drifted from an open

French window. The guests all returned to the party to hear this performance, and Plüschow fell asleep, lulled by the soft music.

Time passed, and footsteps woke him again. This time it was a couple of patrolling policemen on the other side of the wall. Dawn was breaking, and Plüschow decided this garden was not the best place to be lurking. When the coast was clear he leaped over the wall and headed again for Hyde Park, which opened at dawn.

Here he found a bench to lie on and slept until nine. Then he headed down to nearby South Kensington to buy his breakfast. Tucking into a bacon and egg sandwich, he began to feel that his escape was all going rather well. But then he heard a cry that made his blood turn to ice.

"Readallllabaaaahhht it!" yelled a paper boy. "German officers in camp breakout!"

Next to the boy a huge poster carried news of his escape.

Plüschow bought a paper and scuttled onto the underground to read it. Trefftz had been caught the previous day, so the police were now concentrating all their efforts on finding Plüschow. The description it gave made him feel even more uncomfortable:

"He is particularly smart and dapper in appearance, has very good teeth, which he shows somewhat prominently when talking or smiling, is very English in manner and knows this country well."

Ordinarily, he would have been flattered by such a description, but this was all too accurate. Knowing he might be recognized at any time made Plüschow extremely nervous. He would have to change his appearance at once.

The overcoat was the first thing to go. Plüschow was so fond of it he couldn't bear to throw it away. So, rather foolishly, he took it to a cloakroom at Blackfriars Station. When he handed it over the attendant asked him his name. By now he was badly flustered and fearful of being arrested at any second. His anxiety got the better of him, and he replied in German.

"Meinen?" (meaning "Mine?")

"Oh, I see," said the attendant, mishearing him. "Mr. Mine. M.I.N.E. OK then," and he handed over a receipt.

Two policemen nearby stared over, wondering why this fashionable young man was looking so terrified. Plüschow headed for the exit and walked towards the Thames. Wandering along the embankment he took off his hat, collar and tie and dropped them discreetly into the river.

Next, he dropped into a general store and bought a tube of Vaseline and a tin of black boot polish. Then, he visited a hat shop to buy a worker's flat cap. Heading into a quiet alley, he mixed the Vaseline and boot polish with coal dust he found on the street, and worked it carefully into his blond hair. He dirtied his tailored suit and scuffed his shoes, and rubbed more coal dust into his new hat.

Placing the cap on his head he caught his reflection in a window. Dashing Kapitänleutnant Gunther Plüschow had gone. Before him stood George Mine – a docker in desperate need of a good bath. Plüschow laughed when he saw himself, but he still looked too brisk and soldierly. He thought he ought to slouch a bit more. He put his hands in his pockets, and spat on the pavement, as he imagined dock workers did. His disguise in place, he ambled back to Hyde Park, trying hard not to revert back to the proud, upright military man he had spent most of his previous life being.

Plüschow had plenty of time to find a safe hiding place before the park closed. Next day, while on a bus, he heard two business men talking about a boat called the *Mecklenburg*, that sailed from Tilbury Docks to Holland at 2:00am every night. He immediately took a train down to Tilbury, which was just outside London, and sure enough, there she was – a sea-going ferry operating a daily service between

London and Holland. Plüschow hid as close to the ship as he dared and waited for nightfall. He tried to sleep to conserve his energy. Getting aboard was not going to be easy.

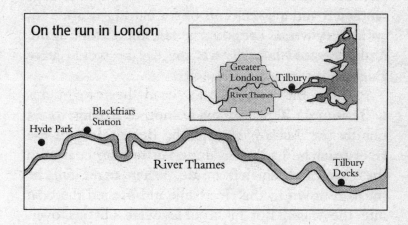

On the run in London

Greater London

Tilbury

River Thames

Hyde Park

Blackfriars Station

River Thames

Tilbury Docks

Around 10.00pm that night Plüschow waded out into the river, but he immediately sank up to his hips in oozing mud. He made a desperate grab for a discarded plank, and saved himself from a horrible death. After struggling out of the mud, he had no energy for another attempt to reach the ship. Plüschow washed his mud-soaked clothes as best he could and sat on the riverbank, shivering in the dark. Very early the next morning, the *Mecklenburg* sailed away without him. Too cold to sleep, Plüschow watched the dark silhouette of the ferry disappear into the distance. He had never felt so miserable in his life.

The next day was scorching hot, and his clothes dried quickly in the morning sun. They smelled terribly musty, and Plüschow congratulated himself again on his authentic dirty docker's disguise! He wandered down to the town to buy a hot sausage sandwich and a sweet cup of tea. Sitting in the sun, wolfing down his breakfast, he felt full of hope again. Today, he told himself, was the day he would leave England for good.

That night Plüschow made another attempt to get out to the *Mecklenburg*. On his travels around the river front he had noticed a small rowing boat with the oars carelessly left inside. When night fell, he sneaked down to the riverbank and pushed the boat into the water. But his troubles were not yet over. Halfway out to the *Mecklenburg* his little boat had filled up with so much water it sank. As he floundered in the river, Plüschow mouthed a silent series of bloodcurdling curses. He threw off his jacket and began to swim towards the ship. Luckily for him, the tide was with him. A less athletic man would have drowned, but all those games of hockey at Donington had kept him fit.

He reached the ferry within ten minutes, and clung to the anchor cable as he got his breath back. Then, summoning his last reserves of strength he pulled himself up onto the ship. His luck held. No one spotted him coming aboard so he found himself a lifeboat and hid under the canvas cover. It was a warm night and when the water had dried from his skin he drifted off into a deep, dreamless sleep.

"PEEEEEEPPPHHH!!!"
Plüschow woke with a start. Was that a police whistle? Had they caught him? Then it came again.
"PEEEEEEPPPHHH!!!"
No, he realized, it was the ship's horn. He peered out of his canvas cover to see that the *Mecklenburg* was about to dock in the port of Rotterdam in Holland. He'd done it!

Feeling all too pleased with himself, Plüschow pulled out his knife, sliced open the canvas above his head, and slowly stood up, revealing himself to all. Much to his surprise, no one took the slightest bit of notice of him. The crew was busy preparing to dock, and the passengers were rounding up their luggage. This was probably a good thing. Plüschow looked absolutely filthy, which might easily have aroused people's suspicions. Had they not been so preoccupied, he could well have been arrested on the spot and sent back to England.

Feeling slightly foolish, Plüschow crouched beneath the covers again, and waited until the last of the passengers were getting off the boat. He mingled with them, probably being mistaken for a particularly dirty member of the ship's crew. Once on the quay side he headed for a door marked "Exit forbidden," and then he was free.

Strolling into the town, he booked himself into a hotel, had a long bath and ate a meal big enough for three. The next day he caught a train back to Germany. After an extraordinary nine months since his escape from China, Gunther Plüschow was once again ready to fight for his country.

After the escape

Plüschow seems like a comic book hero from another age, and it seems oddly fitting that in later life he would also meet a heroic death. On his return home from England in 1915, he was awarded the Iron Cross medal for bravery, which was presented to him personally by Kaiser Wilhelm II. He survived the war to write about his adventures in England in the book *My Escape from Donington Hall*, from which much of the information in this account is taken.

After the war he took up another great love – exploration. As a child he had been fascinated by Tierra del Fuego ("The Land of Fire") at the tip of South America. It had a wild, rugged landscape, and was one of the last unexplored places on Earth.

Plüschow became the first man to fly over this land and continued to explore, photograph and film the territory until January 1931.

In that month he and his co-pilot Ernest Dreblow had to make a forced landing with their sea plane, in a desolate lake surrounded by glaciers. The descent badly damaged one of the floats the plane used for its landing gear. In dreadful, freezing conditions Plüschow and Dreblow battled for three days to fix their float. Eventually they managed to take off but soon afterwards the aircraft's wing fell off. Plüschow parachuted from the plane, but his chute failed to open and he fell to his death. The plane crashed into another lake. Dreblow was not killed in the landing, but died of exposure after swimming ashore. Plüschow's flight diary was found with his body and tells of their heroic and tragic attempts to survive.

Escape or die

André Devigny lay on the bed in his small cell at Montluc military prison in Lyon, France. It was August 20th, 1943. He pulled his musty blankets around his head, trying to gain some warmth from the rough, thin material. The light creeping in under his door told him it was morning. Ahead lay another day of interrogation and torture, just like every other day for the last two weeks.

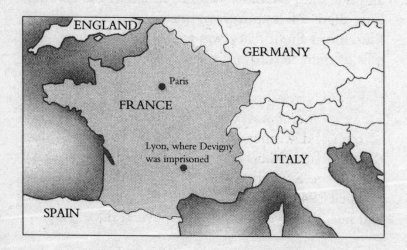

As he drifted in and out of sleep he could hear noises. The prison was waking up. Far away, a door slammed. Guards shouted. Then, closer now, several heavy footsteps and the rattle of keys on a ring. The footsteps stopped outside his door, and the lock was drawn back. As the door opened, bright sunlight spilled in, and Devigny covered his eyes with his hand. Three German guards had come for him. One spoke curtly, in the few words of French he had learned at Montluc.

"Out. Now. Hurry."

But Devigny was not taken away to be tortured. Instead, he was dragged before Gestapo chief Klaus Barbie, and told he was to be shot within the next few days. Bundled back to his cell, he was handcuffed and left with his thoughts. He was 26 years old, and now his life was to be brought to an abrupt end.

Devigny was not surprised by the death sentence. He was a member of the French Resistance – a group of men and women who continued to fight against the German soldiers who had occupied their country during the Second World War. Four months before, in April 1943, Devigny had killed a German spy, and had been betrayed and arrested several days later.

Montluc was where they took him. This grim, grey prison was a last bleak home to thousands of Resistance fighters, and Jewish prisoners who were held here before being transported to extermination camps. No prisoner who entered Montluc had ever escaped.

Devigny was tortured by the Gestapo, the Nazi secret police, but gave away nothing. Once his captors realised he was not going to talk, it was time to kill him. Still, Devigny was not going to go without a fight. But he was weak from imprisonment and torture. How could he break out of such a fortress?

As night fell, Devigny began to plot. A small smile played around his lips. He had a few tricks up his sleeve, and now was the time to play them. He may have been handcuffed, but his cuffs were not a serious problem. When Devigny arrived at Montluc, a fellow prisoner had slipped him a pin and he had soon learned to pick the lock on the cuffs. His jailers had given him a single metal spoon to eat his meals, and he had scraped the edge of the handle on the cold stone floor until it was as sharp as a chisel. Using this, he had quickly discovered he could remove a couple of slats from the bottom of his wooden cell door. While the guards were not making their rounds, he would squeeze out onto the corridor and talk to his fellow prisoners. He had also had a good look around.

Devigny's cell was on the top floor of the prison block. There was a skylight at the end of the corridor which led out onto the roof. Between his cell block and the outside of the prison there was a courtyard, another block, and an outer wall. It was a lot to get through.

On one of his trips out to the corridor Devigny had come across a lamp frame, carelessly left by the prison guards. It was made up of three metal prongs, and would make a perfect grappling hook, if only he had a rope to attach it to. Devigny did not have a rope, but he did have a razor blade – a priceless gift slipped to him by another fellow prisoner. He began to shred some of his clothes and blankets into long, thin strips. He bound these together, along with wire from his mattress, to make a rope strong enough to hold his weight.

Devigny worked long into the night, furiously fighting off the desire to sleep. His head nodded down from time to time, but he struggled on. He told himself there would be time enough to rest during the day, when the guards would take far more interest in what he was doing. He made the rope as long as his shredded clothes and blankets would let him, and hid it under his bed. If the guards had bothered to search his cell they would have found the rope easily enough, but they were confident their handcuffed prisoner would be unable to do anything to escape.

Devigny fell into an exhausted sleep around dawn. Some time later his cell door crashed open, and he woke with a start. He imagined this was a guard detachment, come to take him to the firing squad. Relief swept through him as he realised that it was only another prisoner being delivered to his cell.

One of the guards jeered: "Hey Devigny, you've got some company in your final hours."

The teenage boy who joined him sat sullenly in the corner. After a while, the two of them fell into guarded conversation, sizing each other up. Bit by bit, the newcomer told him his name was Gimenez, and he too had been arrested for working with the Resistance.

This new arrival was a problem. What if Gimenez was a spy, come to make sure Devigny did not escape? What if he was so desperate to avoid torture or execution, he would betray Devigny in the hope of saving his own life? Even if he was none of these things, prison rules at Montluc stated that any prisoner who did not alert the guards to an escape by a cell mate would be shot. If Devigny went, Gimenez would have to come too. There was no other way.

Devigny decided he had no choice but to trust this stranger.

"Look," he said to him quietly, "I've had it here. Any day now..."

He drew a finger across his throat.

"I've worked out a way of getting out, and I've got to go real soon. You'll have to come with me too. They'll shoot you if you stay and don't give me away."

Gimenez looked terrified.

"Of course I won't give you away," he said quickly. His voice sounded tearful, and desperate. "But can't you see I'm in enough trouble already?"

"You're up to your neck, mate," said Devigny. "But don't think they won't torture you, then kill you, because you're young. Come with me. If you stay here, you'll die. If you escape, at least you've got a chance. . ."

Gimenez sighed a deep, troubled sigh.

"OK," he said softly, and the two prisoners fell silent.

So, on the night of August 24th, 1943, Devigny and Gimenez began their escape. The first part was easy. After the guards had settled down, the two prisoners squeezed their way through the already loosened wooden slats on the door and out into the corridor. Next came the skylight. Devigny stood on Gimenez's shoulders and began to force open the glass window. Already he felt weak, and wondered if he had the strength to make such an exhausting escape. But the skylight gave way to a mild heave, and

Devigny hauled himself out onto the roof. Gimenez followed on, making use of the rope.

Standing on the roof, breathing cold, fresh air into their lungs, they both felt an odd sense of freedom. The night was clear, still and moonless – perfect for an escape, with only the prison lights casting a dim glaze over the route before them. The light may have been an advantage, but on a night like this, the slightest sound would carry all too easily, and alert the prison guards. But luck was with them again. A railway ran right past the prison, and every ten minutes goods trains thundered past, their gradual coming and going cloaking the progress of the two men for a good minute or two.

They crept forward to the edge of the block, and looked down onto the courtyard below. By now their eyes had grown used to the dark. The position of the guards was betrayed by the occasional glow of a cigarette end, or the glimmer of a belt buckle or bayonet as it caught in a floodlight. Plotting out the route they would have to take, Devigny saw that one guard stood exactly in their path. This man would have to die.

"Look, this is what we'll do," Devigny whispered to Gimenez. "When the time is right I'll climb down and deal with the guard there, while you wait here. When we can get through, I'll whistle once. So listen out!"

Gimenez looked very afraid.

"If we kill a guard, they'll shoot us on the spot!" he said.

He was swallowing hard, his eyes wide with fear. Devigny spoke firmly, and placed a hand on his companion's shoulders.

"We're dead men already, Gimenez, unless we get out of here."

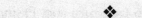

As they stood on the roof the prison clock struck midnight. While the chimes rang out, one group of guards was replaced by another. Low voices muttered cheerless greetings and the new guards settled down to a long, dull night. Devigny and Gimenez looked down unseen for a whole hour, taking in any routine or change of position the guards might make.

The clock struck one. As the single chime faded into the night, a goods train thundered by. It was time to go. Devigny lowered his rope into the gloom. It was so dark he did not even know whether it would touch the ground. When there was no more rope to lower, he swung over the parapet and slithered down the side of the block. He was so jittery he cut his hand on a piece of wire threaded into the rope. But luck was with him. The rope was long enough to take him to the courtyard. There he waited, concealed by black shadows, until another train passed and he raced over to the other side of the yard. Before him, staring in the opposite direction, stood the guard.

Devigny looked at the man with some pity. There he was, bored, restless, waiting for his shift to end, probably longing for a hot breakfast and a comfy bed. But to escape and save his own life, Devigny would have to kill him in cold blood.

The guard turned to face him and Devigny sprang from the shadows. He grabbed him by the throat, and then killed him with his own bayonet.

The dead man was swiftly hauled into the shadows, his leather boots dragging softly on the floor. Devigny waited to see if their struggle had been overheard, but the night was as still and silent as before. He made a low whistle, and Gimenez hurried over to join him. Their path was clear up to the next block, but Devigny was shaking with exhaustion and fear, and too weak to climb the side of the building.

"You'll have to go first," he whispered to Gimenez. "I haven't got the strength to climb."

Gimenez climbed up the building. He passed the rope down to Devigny, who had now realised his companion was essential to his escape, rather than the nuisance he imagined he would be. They hurried across the roof of the block and peered over. They were on the outer edge of the prison. Only a perimeter wall 5m (15ft) away stood between them and freedom.

❖

But as they crouched on the roof, an odd squeaking sound came within earshot.

"What the devil is that?" said Gimenez.

They found out soon enough. Below, circling around the ground between the prison buildings and the wall, was a guard on a bicycle. He made the trip around the prison perimeter every three minutes.

So close to success, Devigny was seized by a desperate need to get the whole escape over with. Their cell lay empty. The skylight to the roof had been opened. Worst of all, a dead man lay in the shadows. Surely, at any time, a prison guard would find some evidence to point to an escape in progress, and raise the alarm? With every passing minute the chance of discovery grew greater. But Devigny kept these thoughts to himself. The last thing he wanted to do was panic Gimenez.

Then, their chances looked even more desperate.

"Listen," said Devigny, "I can hear voices below. There must be a couple of guards beneath us too."

But when the cyclist rode by, the men could see that he was talking to himself. Both breathed a long sign of relief and got ready for the final push.

As the clock struck three, Devigny threw the rope over to the outer wall. The lamp frame grapple gripped the brickwork, and held firm. They tied their end of the rope to a solid chimney stack and prepared to cross. But just at that moment, the guard on the bicycle decided it was time for a rest. He parked his bike right below the men and stood beneath them wheezing.

Devigny and Gimenez could not believe they were so unlucky. Agonizing minutes passed, each man expecting to hear the cry of a guard raising the alarm at any second. In the east a pale light touched the rim of the sky. Soon it would be dawn. But the guard below never did look up to see their rope. He got back on his bike and cycled off.

It was now or never, but the strain was beginning to show all too clearly on the two escapers.

Devigny spoke softly: "You go first, Gimenez, and I'll follow."

"No. . ." said the boy fiercely. "What if the rope breaks? What if I get spotted and shot? What if I fall? You go and I'll follow."

Devigny's patience was at an end, and he snapped: "Go now, or I'll throttle you on the spot."

A fierce, whispered row continued between them. Eventually Devigny threw himself onto the rope and hauled himself over as fast as he could. Gimenez followed swiftly after, and the two edged along the outer wall until they came to a place where it was low enough to the ground to jump down.

Each man dropped with a dull, muffled thump. They were free. The prison had no uniform, so Devigny and Gimenez were able to mingle with workers on their way to the early morning shift at a nearby factory. By the time their empty cell and the dead body of the guard had been discovered, the two prisoners had both vanished into the nearby countryside.

Afterwards

André Devigny escaped to Switzerland, and made his way to North Africa where he joined up with French army forces. After the war, French president General De Gaulle awarded him the prestigious Cross of Liberation medal, and appointed him to a senior post in the French secret service. In 1957, French director Robert Bresson made a film of the escape from Montluc. It was shot at the prison and the actors even used the same rope that Devigny and Gimenez had used. Devigny was hired as an advisor on the film. He retired in 1971, and died in 1999.

Gimenez, his companion in the escape, was not so lucky, and was recaptured. Although his fate is unknown, he was almost certainly executed.

The prison chief Klaus Barbie escaped to Bolivia after the war. He was arrested and brought back to Montluc in 1983. He was tried and sentenced to life imprisonment for war crimes, and died in prison in 1991.

Ten locked doors
(and how to unlock them)

A visitor to Tim Jenkin's cell, at Pretoria Prison in South Africa, would have to pass through no less than ten doors to get to him. Walking through the outer yard they would first go through two doors at the ground floor entrance of the prison, then another inside the hallway. From there, a long corridor would take them through another three doors before they reached a prison guard's office. Then, another corridor led to a door at the base of a stairwell to the first floor. Here they would pass through another door to another long corridor. This was where Jenkin's cell was, along with all the other political prisoners in the jail. Even his cell had an inner and outer door to get through – and every single one of these doors was locked at night.

Any supporter of South Africa's racist apartheid regime could sleep soundly at night knowing that Jenkin was locked up so securely. His "crime" was being a member of the banned African National Congress Party (or ANC), which was fighting for the right for South Africa to be a democracy.

Jenkin had walked that very same route into the prison in June 1978. Now he was one and a half years into a 12 year sentence. Prison life was indescribably boring but it had its compensations. In the same corridor was Stephen Lee, another ANC member, and a friend of Jenkin's since university. Both of them had been plotting an escape since they arrived. They soon discovered that most of their fellow prisoners were reconciled to their sentences and had abandoned any idea of escape. But not Alex Moumbaris. He had been there since 1973. When Jenkin mentioned they were wondering how to get out of the prison, Moumbaris told him that if any escape plans were being hatched, he "would definitely like to be one of the chickens".

Plotting a daring escape made prison life less tedious for Jenkin. But Moumbaris was a mixed blessing. While most prisoners were polite and cooperative with the prison guards, he was usually hostile and insolent, and refused to keep his cell tidy. To Moumbaris, the guards were the representatives of a political regime he loathed, and he was not going to let them forget it.

But prisoners who behaved like this were singled out for close supervision, and watched far more suspiciously. Jenkin and Lee persuaded Moumbaris to change his ways and become a model prisoner. Sure enough, the guards began to take far less interest in him and the three could begin to plot an escape in earnest.

They were all now painfully familiar with the day-to-day routine of the prison. But this was actually a tremendous advantage. The three were able to predict almost exactly what their guards would be doing at any particular time of day. They also knew when they were least likely to be disturbed. The guards' meal times, for example, were quiet times when they could almost guarantee they would not be visited. What they also found out was that after 4:30pm in the afternoon, when all the prisoners were locked in the cells for the night, only one guard remained in the prison, in a little office on the ground floor. There was also a guard on a glass-covered catwalk over the courtyard outside the prison, and another who stood outside the main exit, but he did not come on duty until 6:00pm at night.

There seemed to be two options when it came to escape. The first was relatively simple. They could break out of their cell windows, sprint through the prison yard, and climb the 6m (20ft) fence that encircled the prison perimeter. Simple it may have been, but there was also a very high risk of injury or death. For a start, a fierce dog patrolled the yard, trained to sink its teeth into any escaper.

Prisoners were allowed in the yard at certain times of the day, and Jenkin and Moumbaris tried out a few diversionary tactics. Several dogs were used on a weekly rota, and although some of them were prepared to take food from the men, others growled menacingly at even the choicest tidbits.

But there was also another problem with this plan – the armed guard on the catwalk above the yard, which was lit by fiercely bright searchlights during the night. Perhaps they could arrange a distraction to lure him away, but the more they thought about it, the less they felt the simple option was going to work.

So the three turned their thoughts to a more complicated escape. That meant going out the way they had come in. Jenkin's heart sank at the complexity of the task before them. It would take ages to fathom out a way to get past ten locked doors.

Whatever they did had to be fool-proof, as they would only get one chance. If they were caught, providing they weren't killed in the attempt, years would be added to their sentences, and they would be watched much more closely. They might even be transferred to much rougher prisons.

So the three prisoners set about working out how to get through each prison door one at a time, and what better place to start than their own cell doors? Jenkin noted the size of the keyhole and made a painstaking measurement of the shape of the "tumblers" inside, which worked the lock mechanism (see diagram on page 94).

Jenkin worked out the size and shape of the underside of the tumblers by making an impression with a knife, on a blank sheet of paper that he carefully inserted through the keyhole.

There was a workshop in the prison, where inmates spent some of their day making furniture. This gave the three escapers a golden opportunity. They had access to materials to make their keys and the tools to make them too. Even better, the guard who was usually on duty at the workshop was so sleepy and sluggish that Jenkin used to think his brain only flickered to life when he sucked on his pipe.

Gradually, through trial and error, Jenkin managed to construct his first key. First he made the basic shape in the prison workshop, then continued to carve the all important cuts in the "bit" in his cell, with a file he had stolen from the workshop. When the key was finished he made a wonderful discovery – the same key could open every cell door on the corridor.

How a lock works

Inside the lock, levers called tumblers, hold a bolt against a stud, preventing it from moving.

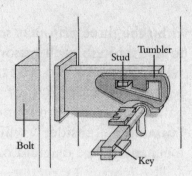

When the key is turned, it lifts the tumblers over the stud.

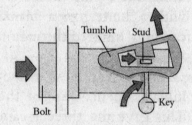

As the key turns, it draws back the bolt, allowing the door to open.

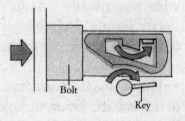

The keys that would unlock the other doors were all around them. They jangled from the guards' belts and jingled in the guards' hands. Jenkin thought their guards deliberately made as much noise as possible with these keys, to torment the prisoners. Whenever he watched a guard lock or unlock his own door he tried to see as much detail as possible of the key that was being used.

The more they planned how to get out of their seemingly impregnable prison, the more they realized there were some extraordinary lapses in security. During the day, prisoners were allowed open access to several parts of the prison, on routes which passed though several of the 10 doors to the entrance. Amazingly, keys were often left in the locks of these doors, only to be removed when the doors were locked at night. To steal a key would be too obvious, but the three men could certainly look at one, and even make an impression of it in a bar of soap, to be copied later.

Some locks never did have keys left in them, but as their knowledge of lock mechanisms increased, Jenkin, Lee and Moumbaris were able to unscrew the lock from the door, or open it on the spot, measure the tumblers, and then put everything back in place. Amazingly, they were never spotted.

One lock that gave them particular trouble was the one on the steel grill that made up the outer door on each of their cells. It could only be locked from the outside. But even this was not an impossible task. Each cell had an open window overlooking the corridor and between them the escapers made an ingenious cranking device from a stolen broom handle, and other parts found in the furniture workshop. The broom key took four painstaking months to perfect, and Moumbaris kept it hidden in several pieces in his cell.

The broom handle key

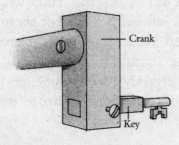

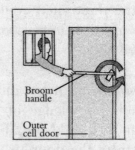

The broom handle key was used to turn the key in the lock, from the window at the side of the cell door.

As their key collection grew they realized that many of the prison locks were very similar. They would find that one key they had would fit another lock, or would need only small adjustments to let it open another door. But the more keys they made, the greater became the problem of hiding them. As with any prison, cells were routinely searched. As far as the guards were concerned Jenkin, Lee and Moumbaris were all model prisoners and none of their cells was searched with any great thoroughness, but the three escapers still had to be very careful. Their keys were hidden in jars of soap powder or sugar, and some were even buried in the prison garden, wrapped in plastic bags, and placed under particular plants so the men would remember where to find them.

Another vital element of the escape was the clothes they would wear. Pretoria Prisoners had a uniform, but the inmates were allowed to order "sportswear", which the three duly did. They also found perfectly wearable jeans and T-shirts among the rags provided by the prison for the inmates to polish the floors.

Hiding these clothes was far more difficult than hiding the keys. But in another stroke of luck, workmen came to repair a shower heater on their corridor and left open a cupboard door that was usually locked. The escapers unscrewed the lock, studied it to make a key, then returned it before a guard noticed it was missing. They now had a good place to keep their clothes and other escape equipment. It was especially handy, because if their things were discovered, the guards would not instantly know who they belonged to.

When they started their escape they thought they had unlimited time to work on their getaway, but it slowly became apparent that this was not the case. When Jenkin first arrived at the prison he had smuggled in some money. They would need this when they escaped, but South Africa's currency was set to change, and this money would soon be out of date.

There were still problems to overcome. Near the front entrance of the prison was an electric door which was operated by a button in the night guard's office. Opening this was going to present special problems. Also, there were two other doors they had not been able to get a look at – one to the corridor on their way to the prison exit, the other, the final outer door to the prison. These they would have to work out on the night of their escape. Maybe one of their keys would fit, but they would also need to bring a selection of files, screwdrivers and chisels stolen from the workshop.

December 11th, 1979 was the day they chose for their escape. That evening the duty officer would be Sergeant Vermeulen. He was the most lackadaisical and dozy guard they could think of. But they would have to be quick. At 6:00pm in the evening, the guard who stood at the entrance to the prison would arrive. That gave them just one and a half hours to make their getaway. . .

At last, the day arrived. Fortunately there was plenty to do to keep their minds off the danger they were facing. The previous week had gone painfully slowly though, and each man had daydreamed about the friends he would be able to see again, and all the different foods he would be able to eat. Years of the dull, bland prison diet had made them all desperate to eat something really tasty.

That afternoon the three arranged their cells, intending to leave no clues behind. They knew sniffer dogs would be sent to trail them, so they washed the clothes they had worn that day, sprayed their beds with deodorant, and sprinkled pepper over the shoes they were leaving behind. All secret plans and letters were flushed down the lavatory. Jenkin found this especially difficult to do. During his long, dark days in prison he had become attached to these mementos of his yearning to escape.

Then, as a final touch, they all made dummies to fit into their beds. They stuffed prison overalls with towels, clothes and books to pad them out, and placed shoes at the bottom of their beds to look like feet.

Their fellow prisoners in the corridor, who all knew of the escape, wished them luck. Some wondered if the guards had discovered their plans and were getting ready to pounce, but there was no reason to suspect this was the case.

At showertime that afternoon, they unlocked the cupboard and arranged their clothes in order, so they could dress quickly. At supper they ate as much of the prison's insipid soup as they could bear, and returned to their cells and waited.

The final routine of the day, where all the doors were locked and the guards left for the night, dragged out. This was a nightly ritual none of them hoped to hear again. As soon as the prison settled down they would put their months of work to the test.

So, at 4:40pm that afternoon, as other Pretorian citizens were thinking about their journey home from the office, or winding down on their factory shift, the escape began. The three all unlocked their inner cell doors with their forged keys, then Moumbaris opened his outer door with the broom handle key. He sprinted down the corridor to release Jenkin and Lee.

Then all three crept to the shower room, to get rid of their uniforms and change into everyday clothes. They put gloves on to ensure they left no fingerprints, and masks, so if a guard spotted them from a distance they could sprint back to their cells without being recognized. Then they ran to the end of the corridor, and opened the door with their third forged key.

Beyond the corridor lay a landing and stairwell. Here on the wall was a fuse box. Jenkin carefully levered it open with a screwdriver and dislodged a fuse. This immediately caused the lights to go out on the first floor. Locking the landing door behind them, the three escapers sprinted down the stairs to the ground floor, and hid in a storage cupboard in the stairwell.

After a pause, as they had all been instructed to do, their fellow prisoners on the first floor began to shout and complain that the lights had been cut off. The night guard Sergeant Vermeulen stirred in his seat. He was deep into a racy novel and in no mood to be disturbed. He lumbered down the hall, past the storage cupboard, and up to the first floor.

"Pipe down, Pipe down," he called out. "Now what's the trouble?"

On the first floor he found out soon enough.

"Shut up, shut up. It's only a blown fuse. Now calm down you lot, I'll soon have it fixed."

The cries continued. Vermeulen wondered why the prisoners seemed so agitated tonight. He fixed the fuse quickly enough and the floor lights flickered back into life. Then he spent a good five minutes wandering up and down the corridor, banging on the steel cell doors of prisoners who were still shouting, and trying to settle everyone down.

The plan was working perfectly. While Vermeulen bullied and barked at the first floor prisoners, Jenkin, Lee and Moumbaris had carefully slid from their hiding place and hurled through yet another door at the end of the stairwell, which Vermeulen had left open. Next stop was Vermeulen's office. The three burst in, their eyes frantically searching for the button that would open the electrically operated door to the hallway of the prison. They found it soon enough and pressed. In the distance they heard a slight click.

Another three doors lay between them and the electric door they had just unlocked. The first two were sandwiched right next to each other, and they were quickly opened with forged keys. Door number seven was more of a problem. This one, none of them had been able to test before, so they had brought three keys along which they thought might fit it. The three men gathered around, and Jenkin tried the lock. This was a hurdle which would make or break their escape, and all three felt a sickening anxiety as they fumbled with the keys.

Jenkin cursed quietly as the first key refused to turn in the lock.

"One down, two to go."

The second key slotted in and turned all the way, and the bolt slid back with a quiet click. The escapers wanted to hoot in triumph, but by now Vermeulen would be back in his little office, so they waved clenched fists in the air instead, grinning wildly.

Door number eight – the one operated by the electric switch, lay invitingly ajar down the corridor, and the three rushed through it into the outer hall of the prison.

Two more locks to go. . .

Door nine, leading to the final exit, was no problem. It was opened with a key already forged for a previous door. Now one lock lay between them and freedom.

This final door was one that none of them had had the chance to test, and it was here their run of good luck finally deserted them. They found to their mounting horror that none of the keys worked. The fact that this door was a plain, ordinary wooden door, with a plain, ordinary household lock, seemed even more aggravating – all the other doors they had come through were huge, solid steel prison doors.

Time was rapidly becoming a problem too. Over an hour had passed since the three had begun their escape, and soon it would be 6:00pm. Having a guard right outside the door was certainly going to make escaping a lot more difficult.

With all the keys tried and failed, it was time to resort to brute force. Moumbaris asked for a chisel and began digging away at the door frame around the lock. Jenkin watched him with some disappointment. If everything had gone exactly to plan, it would have looked like the three men had vanished into thin air. They had locked all the doors behind them, so there would have been no indication of how they had escaped at all. Now, if they did get out, the prison authorities would be presented with an untidy pile of wood chippings and a big gouge in the door – quite a clue when it came to establishing how the three men had got out of the prison. . .

After chipping away, Moumbaris would try to bend back the lock mechanism, but each time it refused to budge, making a terrible clank when the screwdriver he dug into it slipped. Every time this

The escape route

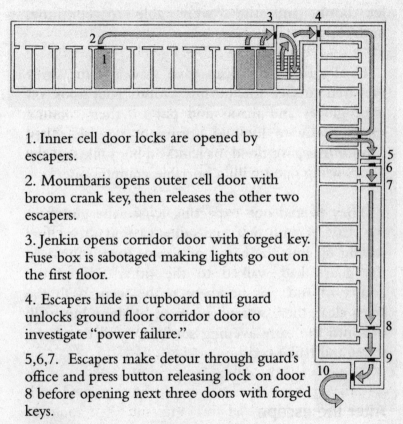

1. Inner cell door locks are opened by escapers.

2. Moumbaris opens outer cell door with broom crank key, then releases the other two escapers.

3. Jenkin opens corridor door with forged key. Fuse box is sabotaged making lights go out on the first floor.

4. Escapers hide in cupboard until guard unlocks ground floor corridor door to investigate "power failure."

5,6,7. Escapers make detour through guard's office and press button releasing lock on door 8 before opening next three doors with forged keys.

8. Escapers pass through electric lock door, already opened in step 5.

9. Outer hall door is opened using forged key.

10. None of the keys works. The escapers force open the final door and walk out unnoticed into the night.

happened, the three were certain that Vermeulen would hear them. But he was obviously engrossed in his book, and they were able to continue, undisturbed.

Finally, the mechanism gave way, and the three prepared to face the outside world. They took off their gloves and masks and put on their running shoes, trying to look as normal as possible. Then Moumbaris gave the door handle a big yank, and the door swung open with a horrible grating noise.

They peered out, expecting to see the guard on the catwalk, and half expecting to find themselves staring up into the barrel of a gun. But fortunately, the guard had walked to the other side of the courtyard and was nowhere to be seen. With the coast clear, there was no more to be done but walk out into the early evening sunlight, stroll down the street and hail a taxi.

After the escape

A few days later, Jenkin, Lee and Moumbaris had been smuggled out of South Africa to Maputo in nearby Mozambique. From here they all left for Europe. The escape embarrassed the South African government so much they forced one of the prison guards to say he had been bribed to help them.

South Africa's Apartheid regime, which denied black people the right to vote, and other basic human rights, is now a thing of the past. The first multi-racial elections were held in 1994.

After fleeing to London, Tim Jenkin returned to his native South Africa in 1991. He works as a press officer for the ANC in Johannesburg. Steven Lee settled in London, where he found work as an electrician for a national newspaper. Alex Moumbaris went to live in Paris, where he took a job in the computer industry.

Mussolini's mountaintop getaway

Nazi dictator, Adolf Hitler, sat in the sparse conference room of his secret headquarters – the so called "Wolf's Lair" at Rastenburg, hidden away in a dark forest in East Prussia. The German leader was furious. He had just heard that his friend and ally Benito Mussolini, fascist dictator of Italy for the last 20 years, had been toppled from power and kidnapped by his own people.

The news that came in was sketchy, but deeply alarming to Hitler and his fellow Nazis. Mussolini had been popular in Italy, until he had led his country into the Second World War on the side of Nazi Germany. The Italian dictator had intended to conquer fresh territory for a new Italian Empire – one he hoped that would rival the great Roman Empire, two thousand years before. But it was not to be. The Italian people didn't want a war, and many Italian troops were reluctant to fight.

Right from the start the war went badly for Italy. Italian colonies, established in Africa before the war, were quickly lost. Italian troops, sent to help the Germans in their disastrous invasion of Russia, suffered terribly. Then, in the summer of 1943, British, American and other allied troops invaded the south of Italy and were now slowly working their way up to Rome.

On July 25th, 1943, Mussolini was summoned to see the Italian king, Victor Emmanuel III. The king told him the war seemed lost and that he, Mussolini, was now "the most hated man in Italy". Marshall Pietro Badoglio had been made head of state in his place. Mussolini was then arrested, bundled into an ambulance, and driven off to a secret location.

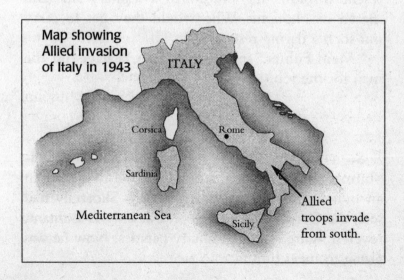

Map showing Allied invasion of Italy in 1943

ITALY

Corsica

Rome

Sardinia

Mediterranean Sea

Sicily

Allied troops invade from south.

Hitler was not just worried about his friend. He was deeply concerned that with Mussolini no longer leading the country, Italy might make peace with Germany's enemies, or even worse, change sides. There were hundreds of thousands of German troops in the country, and they would have to occupy Italy as a hostile force, rather than be there as allies, and this would not help the Germans at all.

The Nazi leader quickly realized that the way to solve the problem was to find Mussolini and help him escape. Once he was free, the Germans could use their soldiers to reinstate him as Italy's leader. But the Italians would know what the Germans would be thinking, and they would be hiding Mussolini very carefully. What Hitler needed was a daring rescue mission. He summoned a military aide and shared his thoughts. Who would they get to carry out such a daring rescue?

"Mein Führer," snapped the aide, "I have just the man for the job."

So it was that on the morning of July 26th, SS-Sturmbannführer Otto Skorzeny stood nervously in an outer office of the "Wolf's Lair". Skorzeny had seen the German leader before, but only as a distant, revered figure at huge military parades. Now he was going to meet him face to face.

The first thing anyone noticed about Skorzeny was his huge size. Tall, and built like an ox, he was an intimidating, imposing figure. The second thing they noticed was the scar on his left cheek. This he had picked up as a student in Vienna. In the 1920s duelling was popular among University students, and Skorzeny had taken part in 15 duels with rivals. He had embraced Hitler's evil Nazi philosophy in the 1920s too, even though the Nazis wanted to ban duelling when they came to power.

Skorzeny came from a long line of military men, and was a natural daredevil and leader. He seemed to be addicted to danger. When the Nazis did come to power and banned duelling, he took up motor racing instead. When the Second World War began Skorzeny joined the SS – a branch of the German military made up of elite Nazi troops. He fought bravely with the infamous Totenkopf (Death's Head) division in Yugoslavia and Russia. But ill health dogged him and he was forced to return to Germany, where he was given the job of setting up a unit of SS commando troops – special units that would carry out unusual, daring and very risky missions. Skorzeny had established his own commando training school, and now he was about to be given the opportunity to show what his men could do.

Hitler greeted Skorzeny with great formality, and told him the startling news of Mussolini's capture and disappearance. The Nazi leader outlined his fear that Italy might surrender. He told Skorzeny that he was to fly to Italy at once and rescue his friend. The plan was to be given the code name *Operation Eiche* (Operation Oak). No risk was too great, for as soon as Mussolini was free, Italy and Germany could continue to fight the war together.

The meeting was over. Skorzeny bowed respectfully, gave a Nazi salute, and was ushered away. He had assured Hitler he would free Mussolini or die in the attempt, and as he walked away he was aware of the fact that he would be taking part in a mission that could change the fate of nations. His mind was already racing, wondering how he could carry out this seemingly impossible task. If he knew where Mussolini was he could plan the escape. But for now, he would have to bide his time, until news of the whereabouts of the deposed Italian leader reached him.

So the waiting began. German spies snooped where they could, and German radio technicians secretly monitored all Italian military radio communications, hoping to pick up clues. The situation was very delicate. To many of the Italian people, especially those who had lost fathers and sons in the war, Mussolini well may have been the "most hated man in Italy", but there were still many Italians, especially in the armed forces, who supported him.

The trail grew hot and cold. At first, Mussolini was taken to the island of Ponza, near to Rome. Then he was transferred to an Italian naval base at La Maddalena, an island off Sardinia. Here Skorzeny planned a daring rescue using high-speed boats, but before he could carry it out Mussolini was moved again, and it was several weeks before another clue gave away his location.

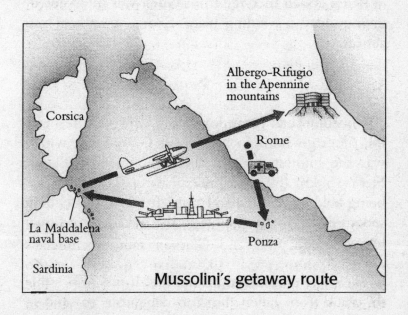

Corsica

Albergo-Rifugio
in the Apennine
mountains

Rome

La Maddalena
naval base

Ponza

Sardinia

Mussolini's getaway route

:, events in Italy had moved on. On
h, 1943, Badoglio's government ordered
its troops to stop fighting against the British and
Americans, and Italy was no longer at war. German
troops in Italy immediately occupied key military
bases, disarmed Italian troops where they could, and
seized Rome. But there was still a grave danger that
Italy would turn against its former allies.

With all this going on around him, Skorzeny had
a change of luck. He had found out that Mussolini
was being held by an Italian General named Gueli.
When a coded message from Gueli was intercepted,
giving away his hiding place, Skorzeny sprang into
action.

Mussolini had been flown to a winter ski resort –
the Albertgo-Rifugio hotel near Gran Sasso, which
was the highest peak in the Apennine mountains.
Here, 130km (80 miles) northeast of Rome, he was
being held by 250 Italian troops. It was a well chosen
spot: remote, and accessible to the outside word only
by cable car.

Skorzeny considered his options. It was impossible
to attack from below, but too dangerous to send in
parachute troops, who would be scattered by high
winds and dashed to pieces on the mountainside. The

only option left was gliders. Gliders were very dangerous too. They were flimsy, clumsy things, but they made no noise. The more he thought about it, the better an idea it seemed. In fact, gliders would be perfect. They would land silently next to the hotel, and his men could rush out and seize Mussolini before the Italian soldiers knew what was happening. At least that was what he hoped.

On September 10th Skorzeny took a flight over the hotel to photograph likely landing spots, and the planning began in earnest. September 12th was chosen as the day of the attack, and an Italian general named Soleti agreed to come along on the mission. He was a supporter of Mussolini and Skorzeny intended him to call out to the Italian troops and order them not to fire.

So, on the morning of the attack, Skorzeny's SS commandos, and a detachment of Luftwaffe (airforce) parachutists gathered on the runway of the Practica di Mare airbase in Rome. As they stood waiting for their gliders to be readied many ate an early lunch, wondering, no doubt, if this would be the last meal they would ever eat.

But before they could board the gliders, American planes swooped over the airfield, dropping bombs on the runway. The troops scattered, and although no one was hurt, the runway now had several large bomb craters in it.

After a brief inspection of the runway Skorzeny decided his planes could still take off, and the attack proceeded as planned. There were twelve gliders and they were soon packed with Skorzeny's men and their equipment, ready to be towed into the air by powerful German bombers. But at 12:30pm, as soon as they begun to take off, things started to go wrong. Two of the gliders hit the new craters and crashed during take-off, including the one Skorzeny had ordered to lead the attack. Now he himself would have to lead the way. Inside his cramped glider, he was wedged into his seat by the equipment he was carrying and could not move to see where they were going. So, he hacked a hole with a bayonet in the flimsy canvas at the side of the glider, to improve his view.

On the journey, another two gliders became seperated from the others in dense cloud and lost their way. Now there were only eight of them left. But after an hour the glider fleet was near to its target. The tow ropes that held the gliders to the bombers were released, and the bombers quickly veered away so the thunderous sound of their engines would not alert the Italian troops below. The gliders swooped silently down to the hotel like strange sinister birds, but as they got closer to the landing site Skorzeny had chosen, he realized it was much smaller and more dangerous than he had thought. It was covered with boulders and sloped steeply down to a deep ravine.

It was too late to go back now, and Skorzeny had promised Hitler he would rescue Mussolini at any cost. He brusquely ordered his pilot to land, and his glider hit the ground and cleaved its way through a rock-strewn meadow. But luck was with him. After a very bumpy landing, his glider came to a halt a mere 18m (60ft) away from the hotel.

Expecting to be cut down at any second by a hail of machine gun fire, Skorzeny and his men quickly poured out of the glider and stormed into the hotel entrance. Amazingly, no shots were fired. Maybe the Italians had been caught completely by surprise? Or maybe General Soleti, who was right behind Skorzeny shouting out that the Italian troops should not shoot, had indeed persuaded them not to defend the hotel.

Inside the hotel, Skorzeny immediately noticed two Italian officers operating a radio set. He kicked it over, smashing it to pieces, and then sprinted up the main hotel staircase. On the first floor, by a stroke of luck, Mussolini was in the first room he entered. Two stunned Italian officers guarding him were quickly overpowered. Now that he had the Italian leader with him, Skorzeny called upon the Italian troops to surrender.

There was a short pause, and then the Italian commanding officer accepted defeat. A white sheet was hung from a hotel window, and an Italian colonel presented Skorzeny with a goblet of red wine. Amazingly, not a shot had been fired in the attack, which had lasted a mere four minutes. In fact, as the Italians surrendered, the last of the gliders were landing outside the hotel. The only dead and injured in this extraordinary mission were the German troops in crashed gliders.

So far so good. Mussolini was now in German hands, but Skorzeny still had to get him away before the alarm was raised and more Italian troops arrived to stop them. This could prove to be just as dangerous as the initial assault. He had originally intended to take the Italian leader off the mountain by the cable car next to the hotel, but now he realized the best way out was to fly. Overhead circled a small Storch reconnaissance plane, which had been sent to overlook the mission from the air. This spindly two-seater plane could land and take-off in a tiny space. If anything was going to get Mussolini off the mountain it was this.

Skorzeny radioed orders for the pilot to come down, and his soldiers frantically cleared away boulders, stones and parts of broken glider from the meadow, to make the landing spot safer. The Storch approached, and landed in front of them. Mussolini squeezed in next to the pilot, and then Skorzeny eased himself in behind him. The pilot strongly protested that the plane was not meant for three people, but Skorzeny felt personally responsible for Mussolini's safety, and was not going to let him out of his sight until both of them had returned to Germany.

The Storch was perilously overloaded. The pilot revved the engine to maximum power, with his brakes on, and Skorzeny's soldiers holding on to the plane to keep it steady. Then the brakes came off, the soldiers let go, and the Storch bumped across the meadow trying to build up speed. Before it was properly airborne, it lurched over the edge of the mountainside and plummeted to the valley below. The ground loomed alarmingly but, fortunately for all of them, the pilot was highly experienced. As the plane picked up speed, he eased it out of its near-fatal dive, and climbed above the mountains, heading for Rome.

Crammed into the small cockpit, Skorzeny spent an uncomfortable flight straining to hear the Italian dictator over the noise of the aircraft engine, as he raged against his former captors. Only when the Storch's wheels hit the runway of the German airforce base in Rome did Skorzeny finally relax. He had promised Hitler he would rescue his friend. Now here he was, sitting next to the Italian dictator, safe in German hands, and both of them were alive to tell the tale.

Afterwards

Once they had reached Rome, Mussolini and Skorzeny took a larger plane on to Vienna, and from there on to Hitler's Wolf's Lair headquarters in East Prussia. Hitler was at the airport waiting to greet them when they arrived. He was overjoyed to see his friend again.

But Mussolini's escape merely prolonged Italy's misfortunes in the war, and did not prevent Marshall Badoglio's government from changing sides in October, 1943. Ironically, the escape sealed Mussolini's fate too. When they met in East Prussia, Hitler was shocked at how old and dejected the Italian dictator looked. He seemed to have shrunk and become almost unrecognizable. Hitler was disappointed to see that Mussolini had also lost his appetite for power. All he wanted to do was go home to his family in Romagna and retire. But Hitler would have none of this.

With so many troops in Italy, particularly in the north, Germany was able to hold onto much of the country, and a reluctant Mussolini was set up as leader of a fascist republic in the north. He grew to hate Hitler, and for the rest of the war he remained little more than a German puppet. When the war ended he was captured by Italian guerrillas. As they placed him before a firing squad, he regained some of the spirit that had driven him to rule the country for 20 years. He unbuttoned his shirt and defiantly told his executioners to shoot him in the chest.

After his death, his body was taken to Milan and hung upside down in the main square. Hitler was determined that his remains would not meet a similar fate. With Germany on the brink of defeat, he shot himself and left orders for his body to be burned.

The raid at Gran Sasso brought Otto Skorzeny instant fame. In Germany his daring rescue made him a national hero, but to his enemies he became "the most diabolically clever man in Germany". Skorzeny led several other daring missions before the war ended, including one in northern Europe where English-speaking German troops, wearing American uniforms and driving captured tanks and jeeps, spread panic among the Allied front line troops.

After the war, Skorzeny continued to lend his special talents to evil forces. Like many former Nazis he made his way to South America, where he helped to organize the Argentinean police into the most brutal force in South America. He was also said to have been involved with the "Odessa" organization, which smuggled former Nazi war criminals to countries in South America, where they would not be prosecuted for their crimes.

He eventually settled in Spain, which at the time was another fascist country sympathetic to former Nazis. Here he became a successful engineering consultant. He died in 1975, after a long, painful illness.

No escape from Devil's Island

In the past, thousands of convicts from France were sent to prison camps in French Guiana, also known as Devil's Island. The main character in this story is fictitious, but all the events and circumstances described here are based directly on conditions in the prison camps and on actual reported incidents.

OK, so I'm a villain. I've done a lot of breaking and entering in my time. We did a villa near Nice in 1905. The owners had gone off on a cruise. The stuff they had in there. . . silver cutlery, a gold clock on the mantelpiece, and those paintings. . . Renoir, Rembrandt, and that modern one, Picasso. I don't know much about that stuff, but my friend Jean-Marie did. And he knew who wanted to buy it on the quiet. Frightening people, most of them, but they paid good money. We made millions of francs from that job. It even made the papers. "Priceless Paintings Vanish in Villa Break-in" said *Le Figaro*.

After that we settled down, and melted into the background. It was a nice life. But one of our gang got drunk in a bar and started bragging about it all. The next thing we know he's down at the police station. The cops beat him up and he told them everything.

The trial was brutal. The police painted us as super villains – really evil. Well, we're not. We might be villains, but we never killed anyone, and we never robbed anyone who wasn't stinking rich. They sent us all out to the prison colony in South America. You've never seen villains 'til you've been out to French Guiana. Some people call the place Devil's Island. . . Those prison camps are the most horrible, stinking, evil places on Earth.

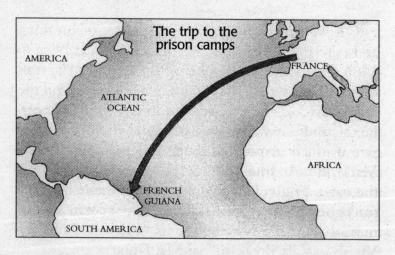

The trip to the prison camps

At the end of the trial we all got ten years apiece, and then another ten on top of that, as "colonists". That's the law. You do your sentence, then you stay there for the same amount of time, as a resident. No one in their right mind would stay in that cess pit voluntarily. That's why they turned it into a prison colony. France took over the country in 1817. No one went out to live there, so they sent convicts instead.

My wife Bernice, I let her go. We got divorced. A lot of couples did that when a man got sent there, even though they still loved each other. I said goodbye to her in 1907, just before they sent me over. We never thought we'd see each other again, and we haven't. My boys, they'll be men now. . . I daren't see them either. They wouldn't give me away to the cops, but someone else might, and I'd kill myself rather than go back there.

The trip over nearly did me in. They send a boat, the *Martinière*, twice a year. They shaved our heads, gave us these striped outfits, and marched us out to the docks at bayonet point. Then they packed us all into cages below decks, 90 at a time. It was horrible. You're fed from a bucket, and hosed down every morning with sea water.

As for my "companions". . . what a lot! Thieves, swindlers, thugs, murderers. Even I would have sent most of them to the guillotine. I went over with

René from our gang. We looked out for each other, but the things we saw. The man in the next bunk got stabbed in the night with a knife through his hammock. We found him in the morning, eyes wide open, stiff as a plank. They say he got robbed of 20,000 francs he'd smuggled on board. Another fellow, a crooked accountant, he went crazy. He started screaming. The guards sprayed him with a hose to calm him down and left him shivering. He got ill, and wouldn't eat or drink. They still left him in the cage though. He died on the morning we got there.

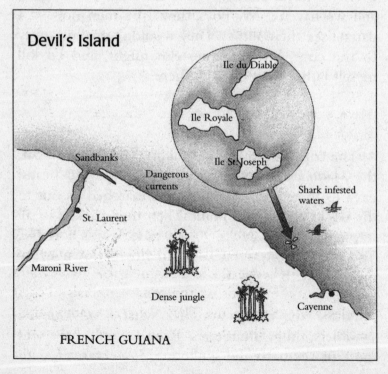

Devil's Island

Ile du Diable

Ile Royale

Ile St Joseph

Sandbanks

Dangerous currents

Shark infested waters

St. Laurent

Maroni River

Dense jungle

Cayenne

FRENCH GUIANA

That's a moment I'll never forget. Eighteen days we spent at sea. There's nothing out of the portholes but flat, dreary ocean. Then, the boat reached the coast. As we made our way up the estuary to St. Laurent, the main town, the air changed. Instead of a salty sea breeze, we got something thicker and sicklier. Air that leached the strength from your body. Air that smelled of disease. We all knew we'd arrived in a hellish place.

I jostled for a look out of the porthole in our cage. The river was wide and I could see the bank about half a mile away. The jungle was an amazing shade of emerald, and so thick you wouldn't believe it.

"I'd hate to think what kind of snakes and insects are slithering around in that," said René.

Every now and then, red and blue parrots would break cover above the trees and shimmer by. As we watched, we saw a huge eagle sweep from the sky and grab one. It was over in a second. It seemed like an omen.

The ship's crew started to look busy as we approached St. Laurent. All along the quay it seemed like the whole town had turned out to meet us. Chinese shopkeepers, the bushmen, the wives and children of the guards, all the prison officials in their spotless, white uniforms. They were all craning their necks towards the ship, curious to see who was arriving.

As we got closer, I saw something that made my flesh creep. Among the crowd were a few ragged scarecrows. . . scrawny, dead-eyed men. Heaven help me, they looked like the walking dead in their tattered clothes, and they were covered head to foot in tattoos. These were prisoners who had survived their time as convicts, and were now serving out their time as colonists. I turned to René and pointed them out. He didn't say anything, but I could see him swallowing hard.

They herded us off the boat and we were marched through the prison gates, which were right next to the dock. We stood there in the main square of the prison, standing stiffly on parade in the stifling heat. There was a guillotine set up in a corner of the square, and I wondered how many times a year that got to do its horrible work.

The prison director was waiting for us. He was a little man in a white suit, and he climbed up the stairs of a platform in front of us and started to speak.

"You're all worthless scum," he said, "sent here to pay for your crimes. If you behave yourselves you'll find life is not too unbearable. If you don't behave, you'll find yourselves in more trouble than you can imagine."

He paused and looked over to the guillotine.

"Most of you here are already thinking about your escape. Well forget it! You'll have plenty of freedom in the camps and town. You'll find the real guards here are the jungle and the sea."

That was that. We were marched off to the prison blocks and allocated a place in a dormitory. René and I got split up, which made me feel very, very anxious.

The first few weeks were a horrible haze, but I learned very quickly. I'm not a big man, but I'm solid. You wouldn't think I'm a pushover, but I had to fight for everything. You'd lose the blanket on your bed if you didn't stick up for yourself.

I don't know which was worse, the night or the day. By day you had to go out in work parties to the jungle, clearing away the trees and the creepers, so they could build roads, or set up farms. That was horrible. Sweat would pour off you, and insects would eat you alive. The guards kicked you or beat you with their rifle butts if you stopped to get your breath back.

I heard tales of men being shot on the spot by guards. These people had the power of life and death. Nothing would be done if they decided to bury you alive. One work party all hanged themselves rather than spend another day working for a guard they called "The Scourge". Some of these guards were psychopaths. One of the prisoners in my dormitory, Henri Bonville, was a history professor who got sent here for murdering his wife. He told me our Emperor Napoleon III set the camps up in 1854. One of Napoleon's courtiers said:

"Who sire, will you find to guard these villains?"

Napoleon said:

"Why my good man, people more villainous than they are!"

And then there were the nights. . . We got locked in our dormitory. It was a huge, long room, and the heat was stifling. I'll never forget the stench of all those people. But the gang fights were the worst. I kept out of that, but barely a night would go by without someone being murdered.

After about six months René and I had found out all we needed to know about the place, and we reckoned it was time to escape. St. Laurent, where we were, was one of the better places to be. You could come and go during the day if you weren't on work duty, but you had to be back at the camp at night. The worst camps were deep in the jungle, and few of the convicts who were sent out there ever came back.

When we got to the colony in 1907, the word around the camp was that Venezuela was the best place to go. It's just up the coast, and they let you stay if they found out you were an escaped convict. At least they did until 1935. Then, the army wanted to get rid of the President, so they paid an escaped convict to kill him. He messed it up, and the President had all the convicts rounded up and returned to the camps.

Dutch Surinam, next to French Guiana, was a good place too, until another escaper burned down a shop that had refused to serve him. After that everyone from the camps got sent straight back. In Brazil they send you straight back if they catch you, but it's such a big place, it's easy to just disappear there. Argentina's good, though. There's lots of work in Buenos Aires for people like us. It's just an awful long way to get there.

René and I thought we'd try for Venezuela, so we hooked up with these two brothers Marcel and Dedé Longueville. They were huge, tattooed thugs. Not ideal companions, but handy if you're in a spot of bother. We all put up money we'd managed to smuggle in, or make while we were there, to buy this boat from a local fisherman. Another man joined us, a Parisian villain called Pascal, and his young friend who was only about eighteen. Then this fellow, Silvere, who was a sailor, joined us. He didn't put up any money. He said his sailing skills would pay for his place on the trip.

So one December night, after we'd been there less than a year, we all made our escape. We slipped away from a work party and hid in the jungle 'til nightfall. Then, before the evening roll call, when they'd notice we were missing, we sneaked down to the Maroni river and into the boat. It was a good boat – well equipped, and with food for the journey. The first bit of the trip was easy. The current was strong and we just slipped away from St. Laurent. The river got wider and wider. The closer we got to the Atlantic Ocean, the stronger the smell of the salty sea. It smelled like freedom, and I just couldn't wait to get away.

But when we got there, things went very, very wrong. The estuary out to the Atlantic is full of sand banks, and we got stuck on one. Dedé went crazy and stabbed the sailor to death. René and I, we knew we were finished from that moment onward, but the Longuevilles were such terrors we didn't like to say anything.

The boat was grounded, and we knew the guards would be out looking for us as soon as they discovered we'd gone. We had a brief, bad-tempered argument about what to do next, and all decided we'd have to head into the jungle. We got out of the boat, and started to wade towards the shore, waist deep in water. I grabbed the box full of food, but a huge wave came in from nowhere and knocked me over. All the food got washed away and Dedé wanted to kill me then and there, but Marcel talked him out of it.

The next few days were a nightmare. We couldn't find a thing to eat in the jungle, apart from a few small crabs on the riverbank, and we were starving. Then Pascal said that he and his friend would head off inland to see what they could find. We all waited by the riverside, hoping they'd come back with something tasty.

The next day, Pascal came back alone. He said he'd lost his friend, but he didn't seem that bothered about it. The Longuevilles would kill you on the spot if you fell out with them, but they had this odd sort of loyalty. They set off to look for the boy. Pascal got really fidgety, and kept telling them it wasn't worth it.

We found out soon enough why Pascal didn't want them to go. The Longuevilles hadn't gone far when they found a corpse. The boy was dead and parts of his body had been eaten. Any fool could see Pascal had killed him. They came back and killed Pascal on the spot, but that night we were all so hungry we cooked up bits of him ourselves. Yes, I did feel guilty, but he deserved it. Besides, if I hadn't eaten him, I wouldn't be talking to you now.

After that we lost heart. We wandered around for a few more days wondering what to do, until the local police caught us and we got sent back to the camp.

Then I went through the worst two years of my life. Escaping was so common, you didn't get sent to the guillotine for it. What you got was worse. They put you in a solitary confinement cell. Four out of five there went crazy or died. The guillotine's quick. You get your head cut off in less than a second, but solitary confinement kills you slowly, second by minute by hour by day. It's the worst kind of torture you could imagine.

You get sent to the island of St. Joseph and stuck in a block with row upon row of tiny cells. They're barely wide enough for you to stretch out your arms. There's a hinged plank for a bed, and an iron door with a hatch big enough for you to stick your head out of. There's a terrible, terrible silence there. No one's allowed to talk, and the guards even wear soft shoes to cut down on the noise. You get just enough food to keep you alive, and that's it.

René and I got two years apiece, but sometimes men get five years. That would kill you just as surely as any guillotine or firing squad. I kept sane by tapping messages out to other convicts and chasing the centipedes that infested my cell. I spent a lot of the time in a sleepy daze, dreaming about girls, and countries I could visit, and my childhood.

I had friends among the convicts who helped clean the block, and they probably saved my life. They smuggled in a coconut every day, and five cigarettes. The coconut kept me healthy, and the cigarettes I rationed out to break up the day. René, he had the same thing, but they found him out a year and a half into his sentence. No coconuts, no cigarettes. Then he got a bad fever and never really recovered. He died just a month before his release date.

I'll never forget the day I walked away from that place. After two years in a tiny cell, I could hardly put one foot in front of the other. People talking — that was frightening, especially when they shouted. And big, big wide-open space. It was bewildering. But I came out even more determined to escape.

This time I was more cautious, and picked my travel companions with a lot more care. After a year I managed to save up enough to join another escape plan. There were five of us this time. We all put up funds for a local fisherman, Bixier des Ages, to take us to Brazil.

It went really well to start with. Des Ages met us where he said he would, we handed over the money, and off we went down the river. Des Ages was a good sailor, and he'd taken us out to the Atlantic Ocean by dawn of the next day. He seemed OK, very quiet and distant. He just sat there puffing his pipe. Then later on the first morning, he said we'd have to sail near the coast, and navigate through some tricky sand banks.

As we got to the sand banks, he told us we'd all have to get out and push the boat over a particularly shallow piece of water. So off we got, and immediately sank in the mud up to our knees. No sooner were we all off the boat than des Ages fired up the motor and pulled away a few feet. We all stood there in the water, wondering what on earth was going on.

Then he went into the cabin and got out a rifle. It was all over so quickly. . . I remember him quite clearly, standing on the side of the deck, pipe in his mouth, calmly picking us all off, very business-like, a shot a piece. He came to me last, and I just stood there, completely frozen, like a rabbit cornered by a snake. Everything seemed to move very slowly.

Everyone around me was dropping in the water, and he pointed the rifle straight at me and his finger squeezed the trigger.

Nothing happened.

Des Ages looked a bit rattled then, and he started to fiddle with the bolt on the gun, and curse to himself.

I turned and waded off as fast as I could through the mud and into the jungle, which came right up to the coast. I expected a bullet in the back of the head at any second, but des Ages must have run out of ammunition. I could hear him laughing. A horrible mocking laugh.

"You run off, you little maggot," he yelled. "There's plenty in the jungle to finish you off."

But this time I was lucky. As I made my way along the coast, I came across a rickety raft made from four barrels lashed together around a couple of ladders. Whoever had been using it even left a paddle next to it. I found out soon enough why they'd abandoned it. As I pushed the raft out to sea, intending to drift with the current away from French Guiana, I was quickly surrounded by sharks. But I'd come too far now to stop.

The sharks circled around me, but they soon got bored and by nightfall I'd almost reached the Brazilian border. There was a small settlement by the coast, and I managed to pilfer a bit of food to keep me going. The next day I slipped into Brazil and headed for Belem, the nearest big town.

With amazing good luck, I arrived in the town during their annual carnival, and there in the street was a costume parade. I passed myself off as a beggar, and no one looked at me twice. After that it was easy. I managed to walk off with some fellow's wallet, and booked myself into a hotel. I got cleaned up, bought some clothes, and soon found work in the town. After a year I had saved up enough to buy a ticket back to France.

So here I am. Back "home". I work in a bakery in Paris, on the ovens at the back of the shop, away from the customers. I live in a small apartment in St. Dennis, near the middle of the city. I like Paris. All that bustle, all those people. Far enough away from my old home in the south to make it unlikely I'll bump into someone I know.

But sometimes I think I never really escaped. I never remarried. I like to keep a distance from people, in case I give myself away. At every street corner, I wonder if someone I know will see me, and betray me.

At home in the evening, or in my bed at night, I'll hear voices outside my apartment. Then I start to shake and shake, and expect a knock at the door. No one comes to visit, so it could only mean the police have found me. I couldn't go back again. That trip on the Martinière, another spell in solitary confinement, and more awful years in the jungle of French Guiana. And do you know, I've been back here 22 years now.

After the escape

Between 1854 and 1937, over 70,000 men were sent to the prison camps of French Guiana. Of that number, over 50,000 attempted to escape, and one in six succeeded. Shipments of convicts stopped shortly before the outbreak of the Second World War. During the war, food supplies from France virtually dried up, and prisoners in the colony suffered terribly from starvation. After the war, the French government decided to close the prison camps and bring back the remaining prisoners to serve their sentences in France.

Bixier des Ages was eventually betrayed by an escaper he failed to kill, and was arrested. He was sentenced to 20 years in the prison camps, but even here he continued to bring grief to the convicts of the colony. He became a turnkey, a trusted prisoner whose job it is to track down escapers.

Several books have been written about life in the camps of French Guiana. The most famous is probably *Papillon*, by ex-convict Henri Charrière, which was made into a famous film of the same name starring Steve McQueen and Dustin Hoffman.

Also from Usborne True Stories

TRUE STORIES
OF
HEROES

Paul Dowswell

His blood ran cold and Perevozchenko
was seized by panic. He knew that his
body was absorbing lethal doses of
radiation, but instead of fleeing he
stayed to search for his colleague.
Peering into the dark through a
broken window that overlooked the
reactor hall, he could see only a mass
of tangled wreckage.

By now he had absorbed so much
radiation he felt as if his whole body
was on fire. But then he remembered
that there were several other men near
to the explosion who might also be
trapped ...

From firefighters battling with a blazing nuclear
reactor to a helicopter rescue team on board a fast-
sinking ship, this is an amazingly vivid collection of
stories about men and women whose extraordinary
courage has captured the imagination of millions.

Also from Usborne True Stories

TRUE SURVIVAL STORIES

Paul Dowswell

As he fell through the floor Griffiths
instinctively grabbed at the bombsight
with both hands, but an immense gust
of freezing air sucked the rest of his
body out of the aircraft. With the wind
and the throb of the Boston's two
engines roaring in his ears, he found
himself halfway out of the plane, legs
and lower body pressed hard against the
fuselage. He yelled at the top of his
voice: "Geeeerrrooooowwww!!!!", but
knew immediately that there was almost
no chance his crewmate could hear him.

From shark attacks and blazing airships to exploding
spacecraft and sinking submarines, these are real
stories of people who have stared death in the face
and lived to tell the tale. Find out what separates the
living from the dead when catastrophe strikes.

TRUE SPY STORIES

Paul Dowswell

"In all your years of fame," Kramer
explained delicately, "you have known
some of the most powerful men in
Europe. Would you consider returning to
Paris now to mingle again with these
influential gentlemen? And, while you're
doing this, might you be able to keep me
informed of anything interesting they
might say?"

Margaretha looked curious but non-
committal.

Kramer went on, "We could pay you well
for this information — say 24,000 francs."

What are real spies like? Some, like beautiful Mata
Hari, are every bit as glamorous as famous fictional
agents such as James Bond. But spies usually live
shadowy double lives, risking prison, torture and
execution for a chance to change history.